CAJUN MARDI GRAS

A HISTORY OF
CHASING CHICKENS AND MAKING GUMBO

DIXIE POCHÉ

FOREWORD BY HERMAN FUSELIER

THE
History
PRESS

Published by The History Press
Charleston, SC
www.historypress.com

Copyright © 2023 by Dixie Poché
All rights reserved

First published 2023

Manufactured in the United States

ISBN 9781467150385

Library of Congress Control Number: 2022944975

To the Huval girls—Alice, Ruth, Genevieve, Susan and Lou Ella. How they have graced our world with their kindness and determination.

CONTENTS

CONTENTS

FOREWORD

Few things say Louisiana like Mardi Gras does. Elaborate parades in New Orleans, with costumed riders throwing beads, doubloons and even coconuts to visitors with the backdrop of music of marching bands that have performed at Super Bowls, are the order of the day.

Decked out in Mardi Gras colors of purple, green and gold, mobs of humanity are shoulder to shoulder on Bourbon Street. Their hurricanes come in tall glasses that carry no warning of the Category 5 hangover and priestly forgiveness that may come the next day.

With Native American and African roots, Mardi Gras Indians dance to chants of "Iko" as they show off months of costume sewing that have blossomed into elaborate works of feathers, jewels and color.

The costumes and parades have a more rustic flavor two hours west of the Crescent City. In this rural region, the opening of squirrel hunting was once a school holiday. Cajun and Creole French can still be heard in grocery stores.

Masked revelers partake in the *Courir de Mardi Gras*, a house-to-house run on horseback where live chickens, which might as well have "gumbo tonight" tattooed on their feathers, are chased through open fields.

A bandwagon of accordion and fiddler players shouting two-steps with French lyrics such as "you left me and hurt my heart" provide the raucous soundtrack.

When the clock strikes midnight on Mardi Gras night, the urban and rural revelry is supposed to end. Ash Wednesday begins, along with Lent, the season of quiet reflection and fasting before Easter.

Some sacrifice during the next forty days with bottom-shelf beer, instead of hard whiskey, and fast on Fridays with crawfish fettuccine and footlong fried shrimp poboys. But just as the Saints and LSU football never wander far from their minds, some are already planning next year's Mardi Gras.

In this book, Dixie Poché runs down a menu of options and memory makers. Besides a history of Mardi Gras, Poché compares the New Orleans with the countryside traditions.

Learn why a tiny, plastic baby is inside king cakes, sweet treats that are always on the table—at homes and businesses—during the season. Cravings go into overdrive as Poché uncovers some hole-in-the-wall eateries. (Spoiler alert: Some of the most scrumptious food in south Louisiana can be found at convenience stores and gas stations.)

Food runs include interesting side trips like the wooden Lorrain Bridge near Lake Charles, a historic shortcut for cowboys on cattle drives, and Fred's Lounge in Mamou, a Cajun music cathedral where beer and dancing fuel Saturday sunrise services.

To paraphrase zydeco great Nathan Williams, if all this fun doesn't make you want to shake a leg, call the undertaker because you must be dead. *Allons Mardi Gras!*

HERMAN FUSELIER is a writer, broadcaster and tourism director living in Opelousas, Louisiana. His Zydeco Stomp radio show airs noon to 3:00 p.m. Central Saturdays on KRVS 88.7 FM and www.krvs.org.

ACKNOWLEDGEMENTS

A tattered costume and funny mask designed and meticulously sewn for me by Jackie Miller from Tee-Mamou garner much attention. When I wear the coordinating, outrageous *capuchon* (ca-poo-shawn) hat, I am nearly six feet tall. I consider myself one of the elite customers to have such an eye-catching getup, as many years ago Jackie also customized a traditional Mardi Gras costume for chef extraordinaire and globetrotting author Anthony Bourdain.

The hospitality shown to me by the Henry family in Mermentau Cove is heartwarming. Their dedication to Cajun traditions has inspired me as they strive to share the French language and keep the Mardi Gras running. Thanks to Herman Fuselier, master of zydeco, author and director of the St. Landry Parish Tourist office, for his suggestions.

Finally, a very special *merci* to photographer extraordinaire/French teacher/Cajun cook/cousin/friend Annette Huval for rising at rooster's crow to follow the runners. Nothing deterred her from sloshing through rain and mud to get the best shots. She has served as a valuable resource about the riches of the Cajun culture.

Numerous communities have participated in the "larger than life" spectacle of *Courir de Mardi Gras* (pronounced coo-rear) through the years. I am sharing vignettes, as there are blurring lines of similarities between the thirty of these runs throughout Acadiana. Many communities have embraced these rural rituals for over one hundred years. Although some

Left: The crawfish net may come in handy! Expect the unexpected during the Courir de Mardi Gras, traditionally held in Louisiana's prairie parishes. *Courtesy of Annette Huval.*

Above: Gumbo is a favored comfort dish in Louisiana. *Courtesy of St. Landry Parish Tourist Commission (info@ cajuntravel.com).*

such activities have lapsed through the years due to wars, lack of resources and volunteers, hurricanes and the pandemic, many hamlets have revived the traditions as new generations take over. Communities such as Lake Arthur, Hathaway, LeJeune Cove, Elton, Daurade and Ossun have hosted runners cavorting from house to house to enjoy a bit of the past. Aside from the pajama-like, fringed costumes in a riot of colors and patterns, capuchons and scary masks, there is a common element of speaking and singing in French. The participants share spirited performances as they enjoy the fun-loving "last hurrah" before Lent begins.

All for the love of gumbo, where many hands stir the pot.

GUMBO AND THE MARDI GRAS

The stage is set for a much-loved tradition of the Cajun culture. It's how we do Mardi Gras in rural areas, though I was not exposed to this type of carnival celebration while growing up. This annual begging for gumbo ingredients or small monetary donations and the wild activities of chasing chickens were concentrated farther west from where I grew up. Louisiana's prairie parishes served as the background within a landscape of crawfish ponds and rice fields.

My personal Mardi Gras experiences included watching high school bands and baton squads marching along colorful floats through a couple of parades in downtown Lafayette. Weather could be unpredictable, as for some years, the Mardi Gras had the sun beating down on us as we reached up to catch fancy beads. Some years, we weathered icy weather and sipped on hot cocoa instead of ice cream at Borden's Ice Cream Shop.

As an unsuspecting ingenue, I finally traveled to Acadia Parish and was thrown into the Courir de Mardi Gras. It proved amusing and spirited, and I became mesmerized by the rockin' roll of a good time. The strangely costumed runners opened my purse and peeked inside. They tied my shoestrings together so that I would trip if I walked. As I was invited to smell the flower on their lapel, I was unceremoniously squirted with water. Rubber snakes were tossed at me. As the maskers frolicked through the crowd, they began waltzing with me and twirled me around. And when I spotted a group of three runners standing perfectly balanced atop the back of a horse, I knew I was smitten with this country version of Mardi Gras. And that was the tamer stuff! Yet I recognized that it was all in innocent fun.

Many of the masked revelers asked me for *cinq sous* (five cents). Much in our state is tied to Mardi Gras—the quest for making merry before the Lenten season begins, the parades, the costumes and the food. Oh, the gumbo!

Gumbo transports me to the setting of my childhood. Gumbo bowls were set out on the kitchen table for sampling the savory dish of chicken and sausage gumbo. Within my family, we all had our favorite bowls; mine—green trim and scalloped edges with a chip or two—had been passed on to us from my grandmother's home. The old, prized hen from my mother's yard was the guest of honor and used as a key part of a day of slow-cooking gumbo. A small spoonful of

The brave fowl plays an integral part in the Courir de Mardi Gras. *Courtesy of Roby Poché.*

filé powder was added into the steaming bowl of goodness served with just the right portion of chicken meat falling off the bone, a wedge of tasso and a bit of smoked sausage to guarantee a delicious meal. French bread was served on the side for dipping.

My mother was dressed in one of her favorite aprons—a faded one she wore while cooking or a fresher, dainty one for serving the family meal.

Even working within a small kitchen, she made good use of every inch of counter space for prepping. Her staging of every task was organized beautifully. There was no recipe to follow, as she knew how to handle it—repeatedly with cayenne pepper in one hand and a wooden spoon in the other. Her recipe for gumbo was a sprinkling of this, a handful of that and better check the freezer for whatever else we can throw in for this one-pot wonder. Okra ready for picking from the garden? Shrimp from Delcambre? And that was her hodge-podge recipe, as nothing was written down. Grab some green onions and bell peppers from the garden and start chopping.

This cozy aura proved to be the best spot for family time through kitchen table discussions. Pen to paper, my sisters and I worked on our homework while my mother multitasked from checking the simmering pot to filling up the Hitachi rice cooker to prepare fluffy rice.

She shared heartwarming anecdotes about her own childhood, growing up among a large, close-knit family on a farm. Since her father raised chickens and pigs, we had ample resources to have gumbo often simmering on the stove. Sometimes, an uncle would deliver ducks to my grandparents after a successful hunt. Folks were generous and often shared their own bounty. You see, so much joy was experienced by sharing. The gumbo, of course, was the best—but it was just one, of which there were many, way my mother showed her love. Her techniques were old-school, as she had learned the basics of cooking along with her four sisters and three brothers while she was growing up in a cypress cabin with a primitive kitchen.

A petite, blue-eyed beauty, *ma mère* often sang while she was at the helm at the stove. And she did have a lovely voice, with her songs ranging from church music to Cajun French tunes and country western favorites. It was obvious that she enjoyed cooking for her folks, her daughters and later her grandchildren and great-grandchildren.

Often when my mother cooked for her own family, the kitchen windows were raised and curtains stirred to welcome in a breeze. As the aroma of a tasty gumbo permeated down the road, our neighbors, who were all relatives, may have envied what we were having for dinner, or supper, as my mother called it. And dessert, it was likely blackberry tarts. My mother had her hand in everything from picking the berries to shaping the hand pies.

The white plumed egret contrasts with thickets along the swampland. *Courtesy of Annette Huval.*

A few times, my extended family enjoyed a larger gathering for gumbo at a camp in the Atchafalaya Basin. It wasn't an unusual outing for us, as my grandfather once lived off the land as a trapper and fisherman along nearby Whiskey River. As newlyweds in prior years, he and my grandmother lived in a houseboat, which I now envy for their adventurous lifestyle. For our journey to the family camp, we crammed into the bed of my uncle's red Ford truck and drove slowly, rattling along on the levee road to get to the boat launch. Once puttering in the basin waters, our boat led us through a ghostly wisp of fog and a wilderness of gators and water moccasins. Riding the boat was the only way to and from civilization. We had the time of our lives!

The rough-hewn camp had a tin roof and was built up on pillars. When the water level was high, we could more easily jump from the boat onto the deck of the cabin. If the water was low, we embarked from the bank and climbed rickety steps up to the patchwork kind of two-room cabin. Tall, mismatched screened windows kept the skeeters out. A light with a pull chain provided light for the kitchen/dining area. A kerosene lamp sat on a wooden crate in the corner.

The makeshift kitchen had a sink and small stove. Recycled margarine tubs were stacked to fill up with leftovers after the feast so that each family could take home a serving of gumbo. A wobbly, hand-me-down kitchen table and benches graced the dining area. We filled up with supplies in ice chests for whatever we needed. Water jugs were set up to collect rainwater on the deck of the cabin.

At the camp, one of my aunts cooked a gumbo of dark roux filled with duck and andouille. Our time with the swarm of cousins at the basin camp kept us all well-rooted. No TV was available at the camp; we had to amuse ourselves in other ways by interacting. Instead, we visited with each other and played the card game *bouree* while my uncles told jokes—often the punchline was in French. Standing on the deck of the cabin, we tried to catch the prettiest dragonflies, called *cigales* in French. The youngsters, myself included, called them "cigars" because we were foolish. We were awed when a white egret flew by. What a contrast this angelic bird presented against the gray mosaic of the wood thicket beyond the riverbank.

Holding cane poles, the kids fished while our sunburned legs swayed over the edge of the deck, teasing the turtles to nibble at our toes. We did not have a competitive nature, for if any of us were lucky enough to catch a fish with the scrawny worms we used for bait, we were excited. The boy cousins playfully swung their poles at each other with hooks dangling. If we caught anything, the bounty of sac a lait was snatched up and scaled by my uncles and prepped by my aunts on the spot. Nothing is as good as fried fish served fresh as an appetizer, leading up to gumbo.

It seemed that our time together stood still among our band of cousins. Our senses came alive with the unforgettable pungent smell of the swamp, tip-tap of light rain on the tin roof, the continuous rat-a-tat-tat of a lone woodpecker and the aroma of onions and sausage sautéing for a gumbo. How our imagination ran wild wondering what lay in the marshland, especially when we listened to the throaty chorus of bullfrogs. As cypress trees seemed to stare at us, we imagined that the shadows of the branches resembled swamp monsters with long arms swaying in the wind. Then we were whisked back to family time. "Gumbo's ready" rang out, and we lined up with bowl and spoon in hand.

Bless the food before us, the family beside us and the love between us.
—Author unknown

CAJUNS INTRO

The group of people who became known as Acadians or "Cajuns" spent difficult years finding a permanent home. In the early 1600s, they were transplanted from rural areas of western France due to distress caused by France's religious wars between Catholics and Protestants. Hardships such as strife, famine and the plague forced many Catholics to leave and seek settling elsewhere. Once uprooted, they sailed to coastal Canada to establish a French colony called Acadie (or Acadia). It is in what is now called Nova Scotia that the Acadians realized their much sought-after freedom. They yearned to be where they would be allowed to follow their Catholic religion while prospering as farmers and fishermen. In their quest for a fulfilling lifestyle, many Acadians—with surnames such as Broussard, Thibodeaux and Guidry—bore large, close-knit families who were dedicated to God and family while enjoying riches of fertile farmland.

Under the Treaty of Utrecht in 1713, France ceded Acadie to England. The Acadians were exiled from Canada for refusing to swear allegiance to the British Crown. They also chose not to acknowledge the king of England as head of their church, as this would be disavowing their Roman Catholic religion.

The people "without a home" faced tremendous hardships once again as families were separated through the massive deportation called Le Grand Derangement. The Acadians were banished: thousands were driven to board ships and relocate along the Eastern Seaboard of North America. This region is considered the present-day states of Maine, Massachusetts,

Children feeding the chickens. *Courtesy of the New York Public Library.*

Connecticut, New York, Pennsylvania, Maryland and South Carolina. Some families returned to Nova Scotia in 1764, though not to their original homes and farms. It was heartbreaking to discover that many of these homesteads had been burned to the ground. Once again, the Acadians had to begin life anew. Still others ended up in the Caribbean French colony of St. Domingue, which is present-day Haiti.

Eventually, many uprooted their lives again in hope of finding a better life. A large contingent traveled to southern Louisiana, a former French territory that had been ceded to Spain. They aspired to a simple lifestyle maintaining their Catholic religion and French language. They adapted to an environment of moss-covered trees overlooking bayous and fertile soils of the prairies. While the Cajuns thrived in their lush surroundings, they also enjoyed a unique lifestyle, including developing a blended cuisine. Many of their dishes intermingled distinctive influences from other cultures within Louisiana, namely Spanish, German, Italian, Creole, Native American and African. Ever resourceful, the Acadians used their ancestral recipes while also introducing the fruits of their new terrain. They flourished by growing crops on land along the bayous. They also hunted for rabbits, squirrels and deer. Fishing and gathering herbs in the wild also proved valuable resources for feeding their families.

Having been earlier exposed to a colder environment in Nova Scotia as compared to the heat and humidity of Louisiana, the Acadians had learned much from the MicMac Indians of southeast Canada. The humble Acadians adapted to living off the land as they cherished the natural resources of farmland and waterways. The MicMacs introduced Acadians to preparing meals of beaver, otter, rabbits, partridge and moose in Canada. Their cooking style included roasting meat and fowl over a fire. Exposure to these rustic cooking methods in Canada later proved valuable to the Acadians in their Louisiana forests and bayou land.

LOUISIANA SOCIAL EVENTS

KEEPING COMPANY

So many social gatherings are intertwined with a common theme of celebrating Cajun food, music, dance and other activities of kinship. In small farming communities, socializing had its challenges. Because of the distance from farm to farm, isolation could occur. From dawn to dusk, farming families were dedicated to making a living by continually tilling, growing and harvesting crops of rice, cotton and corn. Pigs had to be fed and fattened in time for a communal boucherie (pig slaughter) in wintertime. Cows were milked, eggs picked from the chicken coop and fences repaired. The fruits of labor from home gardens were harvested, pickled, canned and stored. Sundays were dedicated for rest and attending church.

Bal de Maison

On Saturday nights, many families who had a set of amateur musicians in their circle hosted an evening house dance, a *bal de maison*, similar to barn dances of other states with entertainment of folk music and square dancing. Dancing at the Cajun house dance, whether it was to the slower pace of the waltz or the peppy Cajun jig, has always been important in Louisiana for its social interaction. The dance proved to be an enjoyable event among the unmarried so they could, under the watchful eyes of chaperones, begin courtships.

The location of the house dance varied each week. Hosting news was shared in the general area by announcements at church services. Another method of sharing information bore a similarity to the Pony Express in that messengers rode on horseback with a simple stick tied with a red handkerchief. Periodically, the stick was tied to the gate of a farmhouse as a sign that this was the location of the upcoming Saturday night dance, a way of inviting those interested to dress up and get ready for some fun.

To attend a Cajun bal de maison, men traveled on horseback and ladies by wagon, eventually by automobile, to head over to someone's house in anticipation of dancing the night away to the tunes of Cajun French music. Guests dressed in their Sunday best and often carried in a homemade pie or a jar of preserves to present to the host as a hospitality gift. The dance usually took place in the front room, which would be the largest room in the house. Furniture was moved aside to make room for dancing. Depending on the weather, the musicians would informally set up in the front yard. Visiting and dancing could take place in the front room and the front porch. As part of the festivities, in the nearby homestead barn, many men gathered to sample a swig of moonshine, often nicknamed corn liquor, made from the local common field crop.

From dusk to dawn, the Cajun farmer milks cows and repairs fences. On weekends, his family socializes with neighbors through communal boucheries and informal house dances. *Courtesy of The Historic New Orleans Collection, Gift of Mrs. Mildred Gould Norman.*

Even families with little ones in tow attended these dances, although the children were usually put to rest and nestled in an adjoining bedroom. By late evening, they were rocked to sleep. This is where the French term *fais-do-do* derives, meaning to "go to sleep." This may have referred to dancers staying up all night and sometimes falling asleep while dancing. Eventually a *fais-do-do* became considered a "dancing event."

The typical style of many houses in hot, humid Louisiana evolved from materials available, such as the bald cypress, which is Louisiana's state tree. Cypress accommodates Louisiana weather, as it is resistant to moisture and damage by insects. Windows were built in a size from ceiling to floor to allow a welcome breeze through the house. Wooden, working shutters, which could be shut, replaced windowpanes as protection from hurricanes. Raising the dwellings by building on pillars of wood or brick allowed ventilation and provided protection against occasional flooding and insect damage to the wooden houses.

The traditional Acadian cottage had an outside brick chimney. A gabled roof constructed of corrugated tin metal formed cover over the house and porch. Frugal Cajuns used materials readily available such as clay or mud and Spanish moss as a filling for interior walls between the timber frames. This method, called *bousillage*, also helped in keeping a room cool during August while warm in January.

The cottages often had two porches, one in the front and a second one facing the bayou, which served many purposes. Porches were considered an extension of the house or an extra room. The space could also be used as a sleeping area if company arrived. Ascending from the porch was a narrow staircase up to the attic and a loft called a *garçonniere*, which was planned as the sleeping area for boys. *Garçon* is French for "boy."

The front porch was essential to many families for socialization as a place to share stories and as a chaperoned courting area. When family members gathered on the front porch in rocking chairs, this often signaled that company was now welcome and visiting was allowed. Before night fell, the porch was well-lit for elders to perform chores such as shelling peas or mending socks. In the morning, under the shade of adjacent pecan trees, the head of the household would sit on his front porch as he enjoyed a second cup of café au lait at the crack of dawn before endless tasks of running a farm began.

Many houses in the southern United States painted their porch ceilings a sky-blue hue called "haint blue." This tradition derives from beliefs of the Gullah people, descendants of formerly enslaved people from South

Carolina and coastal Georgia. The superstition supported the theory that this shade of blue warded off evil spirits, also known as haints, thus protecting the family inside the home. A haint is a variation of the word *haunt*, which means a wandering spirit. It was believed that the blue color would trick these ghosts into thinking the blue paint was water and keep them away.

BEREAVEMENT CUSTOMS

Although losing a dear one to death can be tragic, it does usually bring a community together to celebrate kinship, offer support and celebrate the person who passed. Before commercial funeral homes were available, at-home wakes meant that the dead were laid out for viewing in a parlor. Family members dressed in black or wore black armbands, mirrors were covered with black shrouds and black wreaths were often placed on front doors. It was customary that out of respect, the newly departed was not left alone from the time of death until the burial. In many Louisiana communities, the tradition of watching over the deceased all day and night continues until today, even in funeral homes. A group rosary was recited to pray for the deceased. Following the burial, in true Cajun style, the gathering turned into a joyous occasion for the community to reconnect over an impromptu feast of favorite Cajun dishes.

BOUCHERIES

Although the Acadians relished the riches of the sea and bayous, the versatility of the precious pig is why so much pork was consumed. Dawn-to-dusk boucheries (pig slaughters) served many purposes, as large families had to be fed. It was also during this communal activity that friends, families and neighbors could get together. It turned into one big party filled with dining, singing, playing, cooking and dancing. Once cool weather began and the date of the boucherie was set, usually by the matriarch, word was spread by word of mouth and assignments of setting up mushroomed. Uncle (*nonc*) inspected his fat pigs to determine which would participate in the boucherie. Aunt (*tante*) picked pecans in preparation for making pralines or baking a treasured pecan praline cake. Cousins helped by baking breadrolls from scratch. Children collected scarlet or peppermint camelias and inserted them in glass Mason jars as centerpieces to decorate

A boucherie (pig slaughter) is a Cajun tradition of kinship and food. *Courtesy of Annette Huval.*

dining tables. And everyone chipped in by peeling lots of potatoes for the side dish of potato salad.

On the boucherie menu were many favorites, including a chicken and sausage gumbo that could feed the crowd. The sausage meat and tasso would derive from the pig. But the other items, like an old hen, rice, onions, bell peppers and celery, had to be gathered. Other family members would prepare dishes to accompany the main courses. Sweet potatoes baked in the skin was a popular side dish. Other standards were black-eyed peas and green beans.

Not so mild-mannered grandmothers (grand-mère or MawMaw) would count the chickens in the yard and determine whose turn it was to be invited to the big event. She would ask one of the youngsters to help her to catch the right hen, though she would step in to wring the neck of the chicken herself and twist it sharply until the neck snapped. In time, the hen stopped flapping around the yard and twitching; then MawMaw would attend to the task of setting the chicken on the chopping block to prepare for cooking the gumbo.

A boucherie always began early in the day. Once the pigs were killed, usually by a shot to the head, virtually every part of the pig from the snout to the tail was used to prepare a dish. These specialties included bacon, ham, sausage, andouille, boudin, pork chops, ponce (stomach) and more.

CHRISTMAS

The household patriarch would tromp to the woods to find a tree suitable to cut down and use as a Christmas tree. Decorations had to be homemade because money was tight. The children would string popcorn for decorating the tree. Also, cloth from old aprons or scrap fabric was cut in strips and tied on cord to craft a colorful garland. Pinecones were collected and used to decorate the tree. Gifts for the children might be oranges or homemade items such as rag dolls, which were made by using scrap fabric to form the body, dress and apron of a small, soft doll. Lace, string and yarn could be used to resemble the hair. Often, frilly handkerchiefs could be folded to the shape of an angel and hung on the Christmas tree. After Papa Noel (Santa Claus) stopped by during the night, the angel served as a gift for little girls. Papa Noel found his way down the Louisiana bayous as he traveled by pirogue pulled by a team of alligators. Gifts were not usually wrapped, as paper was dear.

During Christmas holidays, hours of family time were spent making the sweet treat of taffy, of which the main ingredients are sugar, corn syrup (or cane syrup) and vanilla flavoring. All the kids had a turn at pulling the taffy until it hardened and was no longer sticky and ready to bite into.

COURIR DE MARDI GRAS

Another popular mode of social mingling was the Courir de Mardi Gras runs, which began at sunrise in neighborhoods as many Acadian families lived in proximity to one another. The sojourn to each stop on the planned run was short. The buildup of excitement was shared among cousins, aunts and uncles. Gradually, many of these runs expanded to entice others in the community and finally opened up to visitors to enjoy the craziness.

Every part of the bedlam of the Courir de Mardi Gras has ties to medieval tradition and illustrates the parodying of scholars. Colorfully decorated mortarboard hats, the square-shaped hats with a dangling tassel college graduates wear, were creatively refashioned by carnival fans to mock scholars. These hats are believed to have been introduced during the Middle Ages in Europe, when stonemasons (bricklayers) graduated from apprentice to master mason.

Miter hats, a traditional turban-style hat worn by the pope and bishops in the Catholic Church, were also refashioned for Mardi Gras runs as a way to mock the religious. Wild behavior seems to be acceptable during this time because once Mardi Gras is over, the Lenten season begins. This often means sacrifices or performing small acts of kindness, such as abstaining from meat on Fridays, attending the Friday Way of the Cross or giving up beer for forty days.

Along the countryside, the run turns into a whole day of eager participants riding on horseback or grouped in a communal wagon while singing, dancing, drinking and laughing. Continuous playacting is enjoyed as the runners drop by predetermined farmhouses. Sounds of whooping and French expressions can be heard as the group rides along. A wagon is filled with men flaunting their brightly colored raggedy costumes. Their long arms are draped over the sideboards. No evidence of suppressed mischief here. It's a "no holds barred" event as the runners collaborate on providing entertainment.

At each stop, performances are repeated as a chicken is tossed high in the air and the frantic chase begins. Oftentimes, the krewe brings along their own brood of chickens or guineas to toss. A chicken is cradled within the arms of a jubilant six-foot giant, appearing even taller with his two-foot capuchon, which resembles a dunce hat. He has caught the most chickens that day. This earns him much-coveted bragging rights of his feat. A homemade trophy was also presented to him at the end of the day. The scene is repeated throughout the day, yet at each stop the excitement escalates and playful antics are impromptu.

Dozens of masked marauders with scary masks creep up to the porch of their host. The captain advances to the homes first and asks for permission for his entourage to approach. Once the captain receives an enthusiastic response from the homeowner, he waves the flag alerting his group. The riders on horseback swarm to the entrance and descend from their horses, followed by a wagon of runners. To all appearances, it seems that the whole event is chaotic, and no one knows what will happen next.

Each community presents their run a little differently, which gives an interesting view into our folkways. As Cajun families often lived near one another in familial neighborhoods, they hosted a small Mardi Gras where the men traveled on foot to the farms of extended family members. Through the years, runners journeyed by horseback during an event, which became yet another way to socialize and stay bonded with their cousins. What the communities have in common is their goal to entertain and gather ingredients to make a gumbo. Though the song lyrics may differ by community, the overall intention is to explain through their own poetry that the Mardi Gras beggars are not "malefactors." They are good men; they are just begging for ingredients, and in exchange they will climb on the roof of the barn. They will steal away to the shed and pull out a wheelbarrow to cart around one of the compadres to ride around. A bucket filled with rainwater will serve as a temporary hat. They will do almost anything for a laugh.

The runner gently coaxes spectators to reach in their pockets and pull out money to donate to the cause of preparing a gumbo. Visitors should be prepared and have coins or dollar bills in their pocket as beggars sneak up and request cinq sous (five cents) as they playfully cajole their audience to participate. Stealthily, they approach the crowd with open palms extended, gesturing and asking for small change. Revelers are relentless, and the comical game continues as runners scamper, looking for opportunities to perform outrageously. This is their magical time to dress as someone other than themselves for a day.

WEDDINGS

Everyone loved attending a Cajun wedding reception, where food and traditions were shared. For the *bal de noce*, or wedding dance, friends and families gathered to celebrate the nuptials of the bride and groom. The newlyweds held hands, strolling slowly as the band played a wedding march. The tradition of pinning money on the bride's veil or groom's suit in exchange for a dance continues to this day—often this is collected to pay for the couple's honeymoon. Once the groom has danced with his mother and the bride with her father, everyone at the party is welcomed to select a partner for dancing. It is not uncommon for children to dance as well as for two women to dance together if dancing partners are in short supply. And a feast has been prepared by family members, such as a gumbo to feed everyone, along with chicken salad sandwiches, cracklings and boudin. A white wedding cake is served, and a groom's cake is usually German chocolate, decorated to display the groom's hobby, such as hunting or fishing.

In earlier days, families who lived in remote communities traveled by horse and buggy. For the lovers who were pining to get married, this distance away from the city may have caused a long wait for the proper authority to formally officiate the marriage. One tradition was for the loving couple to "jump over a broom" in front of their family, until a clergyman or justice of the peace was available to make his way to officially marry them. The tradition of jumping the broom in the South began before the Civil War when enslaved Africans were not legally permitted to get married. Thus they would jump over a broomstick to seal their commitment to a partner.

Reenactment of bride and groom during the Courir de Mardi Gras. *Courtesy of Annette Huval.*

Symbolism is tied to this act, as the broom handle represents God. The straw bristles represent the support of the couple's families, and the ribbon around the broom represents the strong ties that bind the couple. At some Cajun weddings, even in modern times, the bride and groom symbolically jump the broom to indicate the sweeping out of the old life and welcoming in a new one.

CITY VERSUS COUNTRY MARDI GRAS BEGINNINGS

Fortune favors the bold
—Virgil

Underneath a canopy of moss-draped trees along twisting bayous, the Acadians settled peacefully in Louisiana. By continuing to honor their Roman Catholic religion, they preserved many of the customs of their mother country, France.

The *Courir de Mardi Gras*, or "Cajun Country Mardi Gras," means "Mardi Gras Run" in French. The country people of Louisiana's prairie parishes have their own rambunctious way of enjoying the final fling of merriment before the forty days of the solemn Lenten season, which involves rules of penance, abstinence and fasting for many Roman Catholics.

How do you define the good ol' fashion tomfoolery of a Mardi Gras run? A runner from Church Point says it's about the thrill of the chase, which can prove tricky as you scramble to grab a squawking, quick-witted chicken. A runner from Eunice explains that it's about becoming someone else for just that one day. And a runner from Basile chimes in, "Let's get wild on this last day of carnival season before Lent begins." One runner from Tee Mamou may fashion his own hat using a crawfish net. A captain from Hathaway stages a performance of flogging runners who have been accused of a misdeed. Approximately thirty communities have hosted the runs through the years. Differences between the communities may seem slight, either by the rules they follow or the timing of the run, as some runs are scheduled

The countryside tractor provides a good backdrop for playing pranks. *Courtesy of Annette Huval.*

on the weekend before the actual day of Fat Tuesday or on Mardi Gras day. The mode of transportation may vary, as some runners are on horseback and some ride in wagons. Gender requirements may differ as well as the version of which Mardi Gras song, masks and costumes are selected.

A markedly different kind of Mardi Gras in the rural communities of Louisiana's prairie parishes is performed as compared to what New Orleans hosts, though neither is tranquil by any means. Similar in at least one aspect of the glam and gaiety of the much-loved New Orleans Mardi Gras, the country Mardi Gras is also based on medieval European adaptations at a time when the thrill of the event included a reversal of social order. It's become a magical way of time travel to transport people to a different time, bringing along a frenzied sense of make believe and reenactment of past traditions. The peasant class may parody the upper echelon. The unusual, simpler masks promise to hide faces and conceal one's identity. This is the time to become someone else and throw away inhibitions.

In addition to the masking, the country Mardi Gras emulates the medieval festival of begging, the *fête de la quémande*. During carnival, it was socially acceptable for the impoverished to walk to the homes of the wealthy. They asked for a charitable donation for money or food in exchange for the performance of a song or a dance. Revelers dressed in colorful, raggedy, homespun costumes become beggars for the day as they travel the countryside stopping along the way at neighbors' farms to beg for ingredients to cook a gumbo for supper. In gratitude for the generosity shown to them, the masked revelers act as jesters of the royal courts reenacting a past time. With unbridled excitement, they perform a variety of humorous antics or, as many say in French, *faire le macaque* (act like a monkey). The top prize in the competition is a live chicken to prepare for the evening's gumbo. Mardi Gras occurs during the winter months on the cusp of springtime, so weather is ideal for the comfort food of chicken and sausage gumbo. The large ensemble of Mardi Gras masqueraders enjoys the fruits of their labor, whether it be a chicken, links of smoked sausage, a bag of rice or home garden peppers and onions.

During elaborate balls in medieval France, fashionable women wore tall conical hats called capuchons. At the opening of the grand procession into the festivities, the religious, represented by bishops and cardinals, wore miter hats and elaborate vestments. Professors followed suit and lined up wearing their mortar board caps and gowns. At the end of this "party train," small groups of the wealthy joyfully threw jeweled bracelets and other souvenirs to the spectators. This pageant correlates with today's Mardi Gras krewe members pretending to show off their wealth by throwing out beads and doubloons from their floats.

Jayhawkers

Some historians see a correlation between Louisiana's masked vigilante groups during the U.S. Civil War and the Courir de Mardi Gras.

Louisiana joined the Confederacy in March 1861, two months after it seceded from the United States. Many Louisiana men joined the Confederate army fervor. As time went by, however, they recognized the hardships and resource deficits. For many, their enthusiasm dwindled as it became clear that the war might last longer than expected. Also, a military draft for all men aged eighteen to thirty-five was passed by the Confederate Congress. Factor in that the majority of the French-Acadian men in southwest Louisiana were farmers and did not own thriving plantations nor did they own slaves prior to the start of the Civil War. Many questioned the purpose of defending the Confederate cause. Disgruntled men hid in swamps to avoid the draft while soldiers deserted their posts. In despair, some soldiers switched their loyalty to the Union. These men were called jayhawkers and often served as vigilantes who were masked, armed and traveled by horseback, primarily during evening hours. Their activities included stealing food, raiding cattle, kidnapping the formerly enslaved and other outlaw activities. Although they certainly did not wear colorful costumes, they did try to conceal their identities for obvious reasons. One of the more visible bands was called the Mermentau Jayhawkers, composed of two hundred men who quickly learned how to hide in the marshes and forests to escape capture.

How did traditions like Mardi Gras evolve to the Bayou State? The Cajuns didn't wake up one morning and declare "Let's have a party!" before the forty-day Lenten season began, although that scenario may not seem so far-fetched. The transition to pulling out fanciful masks and elaborate costumes from their armoires en route to fancy balls was gradual, as joyous rituals were adopted.

Mardi Gras, French for "Shrove Tuesday," is considered the final day of whooping and hollering and enjoying dregs during parades and masquerade balls. The feast of Epiphany, also called Twelfth Night (January 6) is considered the end of Advent and beginning of Carnival season.

The famous ceremonial event of yore stems from the medieval European ritual of celebration and masking. What we now call Mardi Gras was considered a time when it was acceptable to incorporate reversals of the social order by concealing one's identity. By wearing masks and costumes, the humble could parody the elite and act like royalty for the day. The tradition of feasting before the beginning of the forty-day fasting period has taken place since the Middle Ages in Italy and France.

Even Canadians, in the Acadian fishing community of Chéticamp in Cape Breton, Nova Scotia, continue to celebrate a weeklong festival called Mi-Carême, which is similar to Mardi Gras. This merrymaking holiday's name literally means "Mid-Lent," showcasing a brief break from the strictness of the Lenten season. Vibrantly decorated parades roll through the streets as fiddle music plays, and masqueraders provide entertainment. The role of the "runners" is to dress in elaborate costumes and masks while the "watchers" prepare feasts of fudge as well as other local delights. Toss in a bounty of spirits, and you have a real party. Spectators attempt to identify/unmask the masqueraders.

One of the largest cities in the largely Francophone region of Louisiana known as Acadiana is Lafayette. Historians agree that Mardi Gras was first celebrated in Lafayette in 1869. Participants gathered at the parish

The Death Masker. *Courtesy of LSU Museum of Art, Caroline Wogan Durieux Collection.*

courthouse, and as revelers may get rowdy, complaints temporarily halted that downtown location for the festivities.

Members of the police jury became involved and declared that use of the courthouse for Mardi Gras balls and other forms of entertainment could only take place if a payment of fifteen dollars was given. This can be considered today's security deposit for a venue rental and was a sizable amount at that time, so Mardi Gras did not happen in Lafayette in 1870. However, the townspeople continued to speak up and wanted to return to hosting a carnival, as it brought so much joy. In 1871, the new resolution was banished, and the partying returned.

The celebration was customized to reflect local legends and tie into Cajun culture. In the early years, the first carnival ruler was King Attakapas in honor of Lafayette's first Native Americans. King Attakapas arrived in a grand way via an elaborate Southern Pacific locomotive railroad car.

In 1934, King Gabriel and Queen Evangeline joined the greatest party in the world, overseeing citywide celebrations in Lafayette, complete with parades. The pair of rulers were named in honor of the story of lost lovers through poet Henry Wadsworth Longfellow's 1847 story of Acadian lovers Evangeline and Gabriel. Separated from Gabriel during the Acadian exile from Canada, Evangeline died of a broken heart beneath the moss-laden branches of the Evangeline Oak in St. Martinville. The name Evangeline remains popular for newborns as well as businesses and products, in recognition of the tragic heroine. During the 1940s, Mardi Gras was temporarily halted in Lafayette for six years due to World War II.

MARDI GRAS OF NEW ORLEANS

New Orleans's joie de vivre may stem from the enjoyment of delicious foods such as oyster Bienville, powdery beignets, sloppy poboys of every kind and Bananas Foster as well as classic libations such as Sazeracs and Hurricanes, which are treasured Crescent City favorites. Jazz music and voodoo legends make New Orleans a beloved corner of the world and the setting for one of the world's biggest parties.

One can hardly bring up New Orleans without focusing on its elaborate carnival season since the mid-1700s. The Big Easy is filled with bedazzled costumes and celebratory balls. Krewe members who ride the floats of large-scale parades toss beads, shoes and collectible carnival doubloons. The ongoing prattle of "Throw me something, Mister" is heard from start to end of the parade.

In March 1859, a twenty-three-year-old steamboat pilot trainee traveled to New Orleans to experience Mardi Gras in a big way. He found the scenes so outrageous that he shared his encounters through a letter to his sister Paula. Laughable costumes and the silliness of the maskers captivated him. Over twenty years later, he returned to a similar scene in the Creole City, not as a steamboat pilot but as writer, humorist and man-about-town Mark Twain. He was traveling throughout the South to gather material for his upcoming book *Life on the Mississippi*, published 1883. Memories of his earlier times in New Orleans had so captivated him that the book includes his take on the zany sights and the joys of dining and wining in New Orleans.

Tongue in cheek, he describes the amusing spectacles of New Orleans Mardi Gras. In particular, he relays that at the corner of "Good-Children and Tchoupitoulas Streets," the area was packed with giants, monks, clowns and a cornucopia of apparitions in costume. During his tour of the French Quarter, he came upon city squares jammed with visitors and lively music. Through his words, Twain offers an impression of a large chess board in which life-size men and women are dressed as chessmen.

Courir de Mardi Gras in Cajun Country—Let the Games Begin

Mermentau Cove

Hitch your wagon to a star
—Ralph Waldo Emerson

Smack-dab in the prairie land of Acadia Parish, among a cluster of small farms, lies the community of Mermentau Cove. Formed in the early 1800s, it was once known as L'Anse Hibou (Owl Cove) and Webb's Cove in honor of English sea captain John Webb, who settled the cove in 1827. Finally, it retained the town name of Mermentau in honor of Nementou, who was chief of the Attakapas Indians, a champion hunter in area forests.

Tall tales of pirates, smugglers and buried treasure add to the mystique of the area. Stories have been passed down of the pirate Jean Lafitte and his loyal gang who in 1819 were headquartered nearby in Galveston, Texas. It has been said that the marauding pirate traveled to Mermentau River, built a brick vault and placed a kettle of gold inside.

For many years, Acadia Parish Mardi Gras masqueraders have traveled by horseback along the countryside sounding their electrifying yells as they beg for eggs and chickens. Although passenger trains routinely ran to New Orleans, many rural residents chose to stay in their home parish during carnival time.

Mardi Gras in a country setting is an eye-opening, jaw-dropping experience. Dawn begins with a splash of pink hues. Hopefully, sunbeams will radiate the sky to promise a beautiful day. Soon, the Mardi Gras runners don their outrageous costumes of all colors and trickle into lineup for their travels to various farms. Vibrant costumes contrast with the surrounding dusty roads and rustic wagons that will transport them through familiar landscapes to offer cheer and dancing to spectators. The runners appear as silhouettes against the paint-brushed sky. In the backdrop is a red barn, and a chocolate Lab rushes out excitedly to greet riders as they mount their horses.

Le Capitaine appears on the scene wearing a bright satiny cape of gold, purple and green. He sits tall atop a well-worn saddle. His horse of fifteen years scans the sight of color and eager riders. He whinnies as evidence that he is ready to get this show on the road. Le Capitaine is well-equipped with cowboy boots, a cowboy hat, a white flag and a burlap whip. He is primed to lead the troupe of runners on the day's journey. His face brightens as the cold air whips around. It looks like the sun is peeking out after all.

Chance Henry is in his mid-twenties. His vision as a leader/captain for this celebratory ritual is to ensure that the runners under his care are not "malefactors" or evildoers, as they are called in the Mardi Gras song. He has played this role for many years as part of the Cadien Toujours organization.

Before the group of forty-five runners and four captains head out for their day's journey, a Catholic priest blesses the group and asks for safety throughout the day. As part of the procession, a trailer or wagon is assigned to house the ice chests of cold beer and snacks along with a port-o-let. The other trailer houses the runners, along with the set of musicians who play the accordion, fiddle and guitar to lead the group in song. There is an eeriness as geese fly overhead in their V-shaped configuration across tilled fields.

In real life, away from the fairytale of the once-a-year Mardi Gras activities, Chance serves as president of the Acadia Parish Police Jury and is also an independent insurance agent. He aspires to roll up his sleeves and better his home parish. An integral part of that is to preserve his Acadian heritage by learning to speak French, hosting a traditional winter boucherie (pig slaughter) through Cadien Toujours and keeping the Mardi Gras run of older days alive.

A bit of a cowboy, he is well versed in horsemanship, as he has been cowboying since a young age. Not only is he an experienced rider, but he also has a talent at roping.

For Mardi Gras 2021, which occurred on a Saturday morning more than a week before the actual Mardi Gras Day, the average age of the runners was thirty. On occasion, participation is opened up to the younger men beginning at age fifteen. Many of these teens have transitioned into this inherited adventure of Mardi Gras running through their father, uncle or older brothers who also once participated.

Chance follows in the footsteps of his father, Keith Henry, who enjoyed the Mardi Gras when he was younger. At age ten and dressed in a raggedy costume, Chance was initiated in the festivities by joining in a children's run. He proudly rode in a wagon with other youngsters. They stopped at neighboring farms and chased a chicken in preparation for use in cooking a gumbo. At age fifteen, he began participating on horseback in Mardi Gras celebrations of local communities Church Point, Tee Mamou and LeJeune Cove.

Chance's earliest Mardi Gras costume was sewn by his mother, Debbie LeBlanc Henry, and other family members. He envisioned a simple costume made with leftover fabric, so his mother gathered and cut old aprons, shirts and curtains rather than use store-bought fabric. Chance wanted a "crazy quilt" design that she could piecemeal, which she did—the squares were not symmetrical. It is likely that one day Chance's blond son, a country boy like his dad, will take over the flag to lead the Mardi Gras as a captain.

Mardi Gras costumes worn in Mermentau Cove have grown in absurdity through the years. One distinguishable costume has fabric depicting pigs. The runner who dons this porcine costume, all two hundred pounds of him, wears a companion mask with a snout that resembles a pig. Another unusual costume was actually fashioned from squirrel hide. To commemorate the Native American heritage of the area, participating in the Mermentau Cove Mardi Gras is a runner honoring a Native American Indian.

Despite the weather, as occasional rainy days do occur, Chance and his co-captains—Steven Slowly Richard, Donovan Darbonne, Jordy Breaux and Devon Vincent—are well-versed in their duties. The condition of sloppy weather and muddy fields brings another type of adventure as horse hooves stir up splashes of mud. During the run, only Cajun French music is played from the trailer. The runners are not allowed to throw beads to spectators. Don't be surprised to watch them in the process of stealing a boat, a roadside stop sign, a bicycle or a crawfish net; be assured that all is returned the following day.

The mindset of the roguish captains is to keep everyone in line and stay upbeat. It's equally important to remain respectful and keep the day moving, as they have time constraints and commitments such as the gumbo and fais-do-do (dance) in the evening. The event has been fine-tuned through

The Mardi Gras runners entertain their audience in hopes of ingredients for a gumbo. *Courtesy of Annette Huval.*

the years, usually with seven stops planned. Chance and his co-captains continue to participate in Mardi Gras runs in other local communities as an exercise in studying other experiences. By borrowing better parts of other runs, they can improve their own event. One undertaking they chose not to include was a formal parade because they prefer to keep their own community event small and rural.

To partake in the organized endeavor, you don't just show up on the day of the run. Members are required to attend one of the planning meetings. Rules are relayed and must be followed. Much discussion takes place on the topic of how best the runners can act as jesters for the anticipated day. They must learn to chant the Mardi Gras song in French. Each captain has a seemingly ceremonial burlap whip, which represents one important method of controlling the runners and their love for rowdiness. Safety is important throughout the day.

Game is on for the runners as they make every effort to hoodwink the captains by switching from one ragged costume to another. The best Mardi Gras runner for 2021 won a trophy because he accomplished three costume changes for the day. So ornery was he that he stashed extra clothing in his capuchon (dunce hat) to change his appearance by switching costumes. This rascal had the audacity to impersonate the captain by wearing a child-size cape and a tiny cowboy hat, which was way too small for his head. Another ritual is baptism of first timers who perform in the run. One way or another, the new members, symbolically called fish, will be dunked in a pond or a ditch.

In the midst of this cavorting, the mood of the runners becomes somber as they make their traditional stop at the Istre Cemetery near Mermentau Cove. Many family members of the runners are interred at this historic graveyard, which is known for its grave houses. A Catholic priest recites prayers in French to remember the deceased. The brief ceremony on this hallowed ground is reverent; runners remove their masks and hats and kneel on the ground with horses at their side. The runners sing "Amazing Grace" as an accordion is played. Chance and the co-captains have been involved in preserving this historic cemetery. One of the oldest little grave houses belongs to Pierre Henry, Chance's great-grandfather's brother. Through family research, it was discovered that the farmland that Chance and his family live on originally belonged to Pierre Henry.

The Mardi Gras runners continue their journey and repeat their performance at each stop until the sun drops low in the sky. They are dirty and sweaty, though not weary. They have run around chasing chickens and chasing each other, even through the stubble of sugarcane stalks in nearby fields. So quick are they in their quest, it's become difficult to keep track of who the flashes of color belong to. They have climbed trees and danced with everyone they can grab ahold of. After cleaning up, they will get their second

Above: The Mermentau Cove Mardi Gras makes a solemn stop at the historic Istre Cemetery to pay respects to the deceased. *Courtesy of Annette Huval.*

Left: Cracklings are a welcomed snack during the day of the Mardi Gras run. *Courtesy of Annette Huval.*

wind and enjoy the communal gumbo at the Henry barn. Rustic trophies will be given out and Cajun music played. The memories will live on and be revived next year.

KREWE CHIC-A-LA-PIE IN KAPLAN

In treasuring the history of Mardi Gras and hospitality, one unique krewe in Vermilion Parish is famous because it was originally an all-women's group, begun in 1952. It was formed to preserve customs of a French-Acadian Mardi Gras, stemming from a tradition in the late 1800s near what is today the town of Kaplan, an area once known as Cossinade. Activities included the Courir de Mardi Gras in which a masked group led by Le Capitaine stopped at various houses begging for donations of chickens, pigs or money to prepare a huge feast on Mardi Gras night. Everyone wanted to celebrate in a big way late into the night, because the next day would be Ash Wednesday and the beginning of the Lenten season. The name of the krewe comes from an imaginative Mardi Gras rhyme: "Mardi Gras, Mardi Gras, Chic-a-la-Pie, Give me your nose, And I'll make you a pie." Some say that chic-a-la-pie is slang for chewing on a piece of straw. Another version refers to *chic a la paille* as a scarecrow.

During early days, krewe members wore funny masks and ridiculous dress as they rode around in trucks to perform mischievous acts to entertain children as they visited neighbors. In 1956, festivities grew to include a parade with floats made from simple materials like chicken feathers, dyed stockings and Spanish moss for decoration. The krewe's signature symbol is of flowing sheaths of rice, which represent Vermilion Parish's main crop. Queen Jambalaya and King Gumbo ruled over a fanciful ball and other carnival events. That same year, Krewe Chic-a-la-Pie began contributing to a charitable cause that continues to this day.

ADORNMENT

Take a walk on the wild side
—Lou Reed

Many communities in the prairie parishes enjoyed early beginnings as Mardi Gras runners traveled farm to farm on horseback. During wartime, however, the runs were temporarily halted, as many young men were serving their country overseas. Although the runs were suspended for years, they resumed and became popular again. Other challenges faced the runners as horses were stricken with disease, which led to runs conducted by piling men up in trucks rather than on horseback. Gradually, even this dwindled.

Years later, many descendants of the original runners reminisced about the thrills of the Mardi Gras and desired to revitalize their unique tradition. They approached local community leader Dale Trahan. Dialogue between the early runners and Trahan took place in the old community country store, which often served as the heart of the community. Word was shared that funds were needed to support special projects at the local Catholic church.

As ideas were exchanged about the possibilities of raising funds, possible plans were discussed. Likely the plans and initial assignments were sketched out on a brown paper bag with the agreement that starting up the Mardi Gras run again in Mermentau could happen. Members who participated would be required to pay modest dues, and the cinq sous or more generous donations collected at each designated stop could be donated to help the church. Led by Keith Henry, Ray Richard and Dale and Lou Trahan, the Mermentau Mardi Gras was reestablished in 1993.

Through years of mending and sewing for family members, Lou Trahan, Dale's wife, had collected fabric scraps, ribbons, buttons, felt squares and

Cinq sous (five cents) is what the beggar requests. *Courtesy of Annette Huval.*

other bits and pieces. As her husband, her teenage boys and she herself had decided to take on the running and chasing the chickens, she experimented with designing Mardi Gras masks. She would often get lost in the project at hand, as each mask is unique, and allowed her creative side to flourish. By embracing this folk art, she discovered an important way to preserve Cajun traditions. Lou agrees that the masks are "nothing fancy," but they are distinctive and play an important role in disguising one's identity.

On her first attempt at making a mask, Lou cut out a square of screen door wire and held it up gently against her husband's face to shape a pattern by marking space for two eyes and a mouth. Once she had sized it properly, she used felt fabric to line the openings and prevent scratching the masker's face. Edges of the mask were also trimmed with felt. To form the nose, she likes using "pantyhose" material that she stuffs with cotton. These soft-sculpture noses and mouths, some resembling swollen pig noses or puffy mini doughnuts, are Lou's artistic signature. The features she creates are reminiscent of wire masks made in the 1940s. To ensure that the masker keeps his face warm during cool or windy conditions, Lou covers the masks with felt, tassels, buttons, costume jewelry, feathers and other odds and ends, including dried chicken bones. These masks are worn by many runners in the communities of Mermantau, Egan and Lejeune Cove.

Most Mardi Gras runners like to be praised for their acting. Who wore the coolest costume? Who caught the most chickens? Who performed the best comic antics? Lou also began making trophies, which are presented to the runners at the end of the day, when everyone has sobered up and cleaned up and is eating gumbo. Each year, she makes mini version figurines representing the runners. The trophies are eight inches tall, complete with colorful raggedy costumes and capuchons to resemble their counterparts. She has demonstrated her skills to school groups where conversation is limited to Cajun-French only.

LADY IN WAITING—BASILE

It may not be the fairy tale dream of a princess, but for Helena, it was an adventure she aspired to. She grew up in the rural farming community of Basile, the original stomping grounds of many famous Cajun musicians. She had cheered on the Mardi Gras runners who took pleasure in acting foolishly and devising numerous pranks. Mardi Gras is a special day to "let loose." Although neither her father nor brothers had actually done a run, she helped her mother, Agnes, prepare the grand meal of gumbo for the celebratory evening event for many years for the community Mardi Gras. Through the years, many women supported the event, either by preparing the meal or setting up their sewing machines to make costumes. However, it was the men who actually participated in the run.

Along the sidelines, Helena had watched with curiosity as the masqueraders climbed to the rooftops of farmhouses, chased chickens and begged for bags of rice or other foodstuffs. She observed the performance of outrageous antics to amuse spectators. But Helena wanted to join the unbridled frenzy and wildness of the Mardi Gras herself. Transitioning from simply observing the fun to actually joining the run was something that she knew she could do. She understood the driving force behind why people loved participating. The Fat Tuesday lovebug had bitten Helena, and she was determined that she would no longer be a bystander. She stepped forward to play an active role in it and become one of the revelers wearing a crazy and colorful dunce hat.

Her community of Basile began hosting a Courir de Mardi Gras before World War II, and it was a male-dominated affair, with many traveling through the countryside by horse on actual Mardi Gras day, led by Le Capitaine. Helena joined a group of women and began participating in a similar run, though their group performed on the Sunday before Mardi Gras. She has roughhoused and enthusiastically taken an active role in the run for over thirty years.

To conserve resources such as wagon transportation and expenses, the Basile Mardi Gras runners participate as two groups working together on the actual day of Fat Tuesday. Although they share the talent of the musicians and conveniences of the port-a-let wagon and beer wagon, they gather separately on their own trailer.

They work together and share Le Capitaine, although *les femmes* (the women) have female co-captains who control their own group and prevent anyone from breaking the rules. The co-captains wear cowboy hats and flowing capes. Armed with a bullwhip in hand, they are prepared if their team becomes rowdy. As the scene unfolds, the group of women runners entertain at each of the fifteen stops together with the men by employing different dynamics for the performances.

Les femmes have a group numbering thirty-five, and they are competitive in catching the chicken. They also climb trees and roll in the ditches. The women are as energetic as the men. They stop traffic on the highway, dance with people, sing in French and ask for money to buy ingredients to prepare their evening gumbo.

On the day before Mardi Gras, Helena stays busy. She checks that her regalia is ready—she has spent hours cutting the fringe and sewing her costume. The color scheme has varied through the years, so she won't be recognizable to family and friends. Finishing touches are added to her mask. Helena wants to have the most outrageous mask—sporting wild googly eyes—and she mischievously considers ways to cause the most fun-loving trouble and act as the best trickster. When the accordion cranks up, she will give the audience a memorable experience. One of the women in her group likes to disguise herself as a swamp creature and covers her costume and mask with Spanish moss.

Helena is restless with excitement and knows that she needs to be lined up in downtown Basile at seven o'clock in the morning in time for the roll call of participants. She likens the event to being on tour: as an actor, she performs in a play along with other performers in unexpected ways. To amaze the crowds at each stop, Helena has climbed a tree, jumped in a ditch full of rainwater, slipped in a muddy field, chased a chicken with determination to catch it, crawled on hands and knees to beg for cinq sous and mocked unsuspecting spectators by trying to pick their pockets. It has become all part of the playacting. One of her favorite stops is at the local nursing home. There is such joy in sharing the traditions of her community.

After visiting the scheduled stops, the Basile Mardi Gras conducts an informal promenade through the downtown. No beads or tokens are thrown to visitors. The Mardi Gras stroll two by two throughout downtown, not missing a step as they dance with spectators and sing in French their traditional Mardi Gras song, which refers to the joy of a cold little beer. The excitement builds as they sing their whimsical chorus: "*C'est hip, c'est hip, c'est hop, et mon cher de camarade!*" ("It's hip, it's hip, it's hop, and my dear comrade.")

And yet the Mardi Gras does not end with the parade. It follows with a gumbo at the city park, the entertainment of live music and an informal dance.

Along with the sport of running on Mardi Gras Day, the Basile runners have reprised their roles by sharing their performances at the Liberty Theater in Eunice for many years. This gives other spectators the opportunity to see firsthand what this country experience is all about. They have also reenacted their runs at Vermilionville, a living history village in Lafayette.

Flip a Coin—Church Point

It was a friendly way for two communities to compromise on a much-valued tradition of their Cajun culture. Just a short drive from each other, both towns are nationally famous for their Mardi Gras runs. The town of Mamou is known as a popular road trip for Cajun dancers, who flock to the iconic Fred's Lounge. The town of Church Point is known as the Buggy Capital of the World. Community leaders did not want to compete against one another for an audience to their festivities. Many runners wanted to play a part in not just one but a couple of Mardi Gras runs. The scheduling conflicted with dual participation.

In Church Point, the rural Mardi Gras has not changed much from when it was first organized by early settlers. In 1961, it was agreed that a representative from each of these communities would flip a coin. The declared winner would determine which community would host its run on actual Mardi Gras day. The other community would move its celebration to the Sunday prior to Mardi Gras. Thus, both communities could embrace their revelry and share the excitement with visitors.

The result of the coin toss overseen by Senator Paul Tate of Mamou and Elton Richard of Church Point determined that Mamou would conduct its run on Mardi Gras day, and Church Point would take over the weekend prior to Fat Tuesday.

In 1961, Church Point entrepreneur Elton Richard did not want to sit on the sidelines. He wanted to help his community, support local businesses and spearhead a movement to preserve the Cajun culture. Some of his spirit may have derived from the experiences and challenges he faced as a young man in World War II, as he participated in the invasion and liberation of France from the Nazis. He had a big heart and love for his community, so he envisioned a larger Mardi Gras run.

As an experienced horseman, Elton Richard was first captain and carried a cow horn (*corne-a-vache*) to get attention from his runners. Under Richard's guidance as founder and first captain of the Church Point Saddle Tramp Riders Club, which was organized in 1948, a building and campground was built to be used for the annual Mardi Gras as well as other community events. Church Point is known as the Buggy Capital of the World and formerly hosted a festival honoring the tradition of buggies for transportation. Early Church Point Mardi Gras runs did not have wagons filled up with masked men. Instead, only horsemen traveled on the dusty roads for the inaugural Church Point Mardi Gras.

The Church Point Saddle Tramp Riders Club organization supports an annual school essay contest for high school students with the theme of "What Mardi Gras means to me." The best essay writer is awarded a college scholarship. The club also donates to special projects of local churches, the cattlemen's association and the community veterans' park.

The Saturday before Mardi Gras in Church Point is dedicated to children; two hundred kids dress in costume and go wild by chasing a chicken at one stop. Both genders participate in the run, and a family-friendly parade follows. Every year, someone special, such as one of the original organizers of Church Point's Mardi Gras, is honored.

For the main event, which draws worldwide media attention, the runs are composed of miles of wagons filled with costumed and masked runners, all men. Twelve co-captains monitor the convoy with a couple of men scattered from the beginning to the end of the line, called the "caboose." Though unmasked, the captains are distinctive, as they are adorned with a flowing cape of purple, green and gold. They wear cowboy hats and boots as they ride the Louisiana prairie range during the Mardi Gras run.

The event has come a long way—the most recent run drew an estimated fifty thousand visitors from all over the world. It takes a lot of dedicated volunteers to follow safety rules, clean up after horses galloping on the streets, line up the wagons, secure musicians, order port-o-lets and select chickens for the chases. It also takes numerous law enforcers to control vehicle traffic, horse traffic, wagons and runners. Assurances are made that all the runners meet the criteria. They must be masked and costumed in keeping with old customs, pay thirty-five dollars to ride in a wagon and physically participate as a runner. Punctuality for lining up is expected, and participants must sign off on a liability waiver. They are required to adhere to rules, which include no lewd behavior or foul language. Speaking in French is encouraged, and the runners are urged to learn the Mardi Gras chant or song in French. For their dues, the participants receive seven beer tickets for the day and a brown-bagged lunch of boudin and boiled egg. Many of the property owners at designated Mardi Gras stops share additional nourishment with the runners.

The Church Point Courir de Mardi Gras is a favored adventure for photographers, as they unabashedly slosh through the mud and attempt to follow the runners step by step. Everyone looks up as the chicken is tossed in the air. It's a guess which way the barnyard fowl will head. Will it fly or run? An outlandish obstacle race begins as runners jump over and through barbed wire fencing or other challenging conditions to catch the most chickens.

Following the run, a two-hour parade is held in downtown Church Point, beginning at 1:30 p.m. Official T-shirts with rustic Cajun Mardi Gras designs are sold. Beads, other Mardi Gras tokens and jello shots are thrown to visitors, as the runners, many of whom are dirty, sweaty and perhaps a little tipsy, are reinvigorated by the cheers from parade spectators. Leftover beads from the parade are donated to LARC (Lafayette Association of Retarded Citizens) which cleans, recycles and sells the beads as a fundraiser.

FAMILY-FRIENDLY MARDI GRAS

With research through social media and TV announcements, it is possible to create a memorable Mardi Gras with children. Some communities such as Church Point and Tee Mamou sponsor a children's chicken run in a controlled setting of a small group, usually hosted prior to actual Mardi Gras Day. Venues such as Lafayette's Vermilionville and Moncus Park host raggedy-costumed krewes who reenact the singing, silliness and wild ride of the chicken chase. Vermilionville has a wonderful resource on its website www.vermilionville.org from which educational resources may be downloaded. The content is suitable for not only children but also adults to get a summary of the history of the Acadians, Mardi Gras, Louisiana gumbo and much more. Suggested activities are included along with valuable anchor lessons.

Breaux Bridge's Teche Center for the Arts hosts a craft workshop where children may learn how to decorate a Cajun Mardi Gras mask. The Teche Center also hosts a children's Lundi Gras (Fat Monday) procession through downtown Breaux Bridge in which fifty children dressed in fringed costumes, pointed hats and handmade masks carouse through designated spots for parading, dancing, begging for gumbo ingredients and chasing a chicken.

Keep it small for the little ones! A king cake can be served for a children's Mardi Gras party, where all kids can wear paper crowns that they have colored. To keep the kids active, decorating their own king cake cupcakes with frosting and sprinkles can also prove entertaining.

Mardi Gras shoebox floats are a great art project for kids to make. Be mindful that the craft project should be age-appropriate and children are supervised if using scissors or glue.

Basic materials may include the following: a shoe box with lid, scissors, glue, adhesive tape, odds and ends to use for decorating the box such as buttons, rickrack, glitter, ribbon, pom-poms, recycled Mardi Gras beads,

Many children embrace the traditions of the Tee Mamou run. *Courtesy of Annette Huval.*

pipe cleaners and construction, wrapping or crepe paper. A good first step is to wrap the shoebox using glossy wrapping paper in the Mardi Gras colors.

Then turn the creative juices loose as the children decorate the shoeboxes in any fashion. If a tiny someone wants to "ride" the float, Lego® people or plastic dolls and animals can be glued on top of the box in time to have a stunning Mardi Gras shoebox parade.

To recycle the Mardi Gras shoeboxes, they may be filled with sundries such as hand lotion, tissue packs, candy, a pair of socks and other small treats to spread joy by donating to residents of a local nursing home.

MASKS AND COSTUMES

Variety's the very spice of life, That gives it all its flavor.
—William Cowper

Many aspects of Mardi Gras spark exuberance and frivolity during the unique event. The colorful costumes and rustic masks are integral; they lend runners the opportunity to carve out a new identity as part of role reversal. Some masks portray the runner as scary, and some are outrageously funny.

As the marauders fly through dusty roads en route to their next stop, flashes of bright colors fly by as they make ready for their next performance. For a performance it is!

Although the captains leave their faces unmasked, they are suitably costumed in elaborate silky capes representing Mardi Gras. Each rural community, even those just ten miles apart, sponsors treasured Mardi Gras runs with different rules about the masks and costumes the runners sport.

Jackie Miller of the Tee Mamou community, outside of Iota, has been designing and sewing Mardi Gras costumes for over forty years. She is an expert at creating the masks, capuchons and one-of-a-kind fringed costumes.

Tee Mamou masks are distinctive because they traditionally have long noses with a variety of colorful decorations. Jackie uses a double screen for her masks. Her nimble fingers take time to shape the double screen of plastic mesh on the inside and wire on the outside. It's important for the mask wearer to be able to see out of the mask and just as important that the viewers cannot see who is behind the magical mask. In earlier times, masks were decorated by using pinecones, horse tail hair, empty thread spools, moss, acorns, feathers from guineas and whatever could be found in nature. It's a craft Jackie learned on her own as her sons became interested in participating in the runs. Jackie practices creativity by using braid, pom poms, rickrack, felt and pipe cleaners in the masks she makes.

In the early days of her handcraft trials, she used screen from screen doors to form a cone and covered it with colorful fabric to form the capuchon hats. Now she uses a more flexible material such as poster board. One of her more famous customers was roadrunner, chef and author Anthony Bourdain, who traveled to Louisiana in 2018 and participated as a runner in a Courir de Mardi Gras for his show *Parts Unknown*. During this segment, he accurately and humorously compared the country Mardi Gras to "trick or treating" among grown men who have enjoyed beer since early in the day.

Jackie embraced the art of sewing when she was in high school and made good use of her talents when her husband, father-in-law, brother-in-law and eventually her sons became Mardi Gras runners. One of her first experiences face-to-face with the runners was when a group of masked marauders visited her school to perform their antics for the children. It brought a sense of unbridled excitement and wonder of this unusual event. She uses a pajama pattern to fashion loose-fitting two-piece costumes made of cotton fabric—the bottom and a button-up top. Strips of cloth are cut in small rectangles and used as fringing to be sewn onto the sleeves and up and down the legs. The fringing is also sewn on the capuchon. Normally, the runners wear jeans, sweatpants or thermal underwear underneath the official costume. She makes fifteen costumes a year and sixty masks. It takes three hours to cut and sew a costume, including the fringe. The fringe is used to represent the rags of peasants or beggars in keeping with the Courir de Mardi Gras theme. Cotton fabric is used, and the more vibrant, the better. Jackie estimates that it takes forty-five minutes to shape and decorate a screen mask and forty-five minutes to make the capuchon. A short curtain of two-foot-long fabric hangs from the hat, extending from the corner of the eye and all around the back of the neck. The purpose of this well-placed fringe is to hide the appearance of the mask wearer's features. Jackie's creative costumes are considered heirlooms, and some have been displayed as art.

As part of her outreach commitment, Jackie has demonstrated her mask-making skills at Vermilionville, a living history museum in Lafayette. She shows visitors how her masks can appear scary by using exaggerated features such as a long nose with a jingle bell pinned at the end of it and a set of lips made of felt. Jackie has also worked with Teche Center for the Arts in Breaux Bridge teaching kids how to decorate a Mardi Gras screen mask while parents are on hand to help with glue guns to complete the mask. Her demos are more than hands-on as she shares the background of the prairie parishes' Mardi Gras.

Creating these costumes is Jackie's passion. For her husband, Larry, a retired educator, his artistry is making accordions. You won't get lost finding the Miller home and workshop in their rural area, as it is recognizable by the symbol of an accordion posted on the mailbox. Another cultural exchange of their talents was the couple's travels to France twice to demonstrate their individual crafts of making masks and accordions. They also gave cooking demonstrations, which were much appreciated, as they introduced the French to Cajun gumbo.

Their grandson musician Blake Miller is part of the revival of younger high-energy Cajun musicians who have embraced their beloved culture by speaking and singing in French. He is a multi-Grammy-nominated musician and heads the popular group Blake Miller and the Old-Fashioned Aces.

In Tee Mamou, Mardi Gras runs with only men began before World War II. Now, along with a men's group, a women's group participates in a run held on Saturday, also called Samedi Gras or Fat Saturday. A children's group runs on Sunday, while the men run on actual Mardi Gras day. One of the initiation rites for new runners of the male group is to be tossed into a crawfish pond—hopefully he will scoop up a couple of crawfish and chase other runners in fun. One of the unique skits performed during the run is called a "dead man's revival," which originated in France. In this scenario, a runner falls from a tree and dramatically pretends he is dead until the captain staggers over and pours wine on his face to revive him—which it certainly does. And the play continues.

An early patriarch of the Tee Mamou Mardi Gras was the late Gerald Frugé, who is still honored for his dedication to continuing this cultural ritual. A stop at the Reed Cemetery is taken before lunch during the run. The runners and followers pay respect at the gravesite of Gerald Frugé, who died in 1998 and was buried on Ash Wednesday, the first day of the Lenten season.

The runners continue their journey by heading to town by wagon at 2:00 p.m. on Mardi Gras day for the community to enjoy the excitement of zany costumes and continuous playacting. In a festival setting, booths of crafts for sale and a food court are assembled. Cajun music is played. The runners have their own unique Mardi Gras song that refers being "drunk to the dregs."

The grand performance of mischief of the Tee Mamou runners takes place at DI's Cajun restaurant in Basile, where the runners are exuberated, though not inebriated. They pretend to fight with each other and pirouette with customers. Arm in arm they parade into the restaurant and continue to collect coins for their prized gumbo. And baffled spectators have a front-row seat as the crescendo of the Mardi Gras music builds. When Le Capitaine commands that it's time for the evening to end, the runners must exit. They do not want the party to end, so this is the time the runners courageously climb up the rafters and mutiny against their captain as they refuse to leave. The runners are dragged out of the restaurant for all to see. A close tie exists with DI's Restaurant, as it was Gerald's brother Daniel Isaac Frugé who founded the eatery.

DANCING ON A HORSE

All the world's a stage, and all the men and women merely players.
They have their exits and their entrances; and one man in his time
plays many parts.
—William Shakespeare

Like his father before him, Rémy works long hours on a rig in the Gulf of Mexico, as the oil and gas industry has played a key role in Louisiana for over one hundred years. On the job, Rémy wears a hard hat, red coveralls and steel toe boots.

Dancing on a horse. *Courtesy of Annette Huval.*

His grandparents speak French and have often shared much about their long days of working in cotton fields, living on cornbread and milk for supper, surviving floods and wartime and making the treat of tac-tac (popcorn balls) at Christmas. They also instilled in him a love of their Cajun heritage.

His grandfather recounted the early years of Mardi Gras in the country. The young boys participated in a children's run through farmhouse yards, often barefooted. Once the boys became teenagers, they would join the more experienced men on horseback, often riding bareback. Early costumes were primitive. At that time, people could not afford to make fancy costumes and did not have many articles of clothing to fashion into a proper costume, whether for Halloween or Mardi Gras. Hand-me-down suits of jackets and pants were restyled, and colorful patches were added to present a festive appearance. Often the jacket and slacks purposely did not match so the runner resembled a peasant, in keeping with the theme. Old hats were reshaped, as the runners wanted to look outrageous. At one time, inexpensive masks manufactured in China were available for purchase at many small-town general stores in Louisiana.

In early days, once participants were geared appropriately, the act of stopping at various countryside farmhouses was more than a performance. Runners actually needed to gather enough ingredients like rice, sausage, tasso and live chickens to cook enough gumbo to feed a large gathering. Donations of live ducks and guineas as well as eggs and sweet potatoes were also welcomed as the runners traversed along gravel roads or through fields.

Rémy works hard, but he also plays hard. During his free time, he enjoys wintertime hunts with friends near Gueydan, a haven for ducks. For this season, he wears the full gear of camouflage and grows a *Duck Dynasty* beard to stay warm. He is experienced in cleaning ducks he has shot and works with his hunting dogs to retrieve his bounty. He has been told that the duck and andouille gumbo that he frequently cooks at the Pas Bon (French for "Not Good") Camp could win an award for best camp cooking. He has a busy life and looks forward to the weekends. For morning mass on Sundays, he wears his best jeans and western shirt and broken-in cowboy boots. Another part of his routine is to enjoy family time when his mother cooks pork stew and rice and gravy, and his sister bakes a fig preserve cake. One of his brothers is learning how to play the fiddle, so the whole family, noticeably kids and grandkids, listens intently. Although Rémy doesn't speak French fluently, he deciphers most of what his older family members are saying. He hears French spoken in the community at most local boudin spots. And he listens to French music at local watering holes.

Downtown Eunice horse parade. *Courtesy of David Simpson through St. Landry Parish Tourist Commission.*

In his community of Eunice, Rémy loves this style of Cajun Mardi Gras. The carnival season is like Christmas for him, as the normal routine of life is cast aside. There is more to this dude than what meets the eye. He has a couple of colorful costumes handmade for him by local seamstresses through the years. He can switch the costumes around so he won't be recognized and can remain anonymous and be mischievous. He may look like a ragamuffin, as his costumes are not glittery or suitable for fancy parades like in New Orleans. His hometown is a three-hour drive from New Orleans, the mecca of Mardi Gras. Simple raggedy costumes such as his are those of the country Mardi Gras. His capuchon and costume do not match. His favorite screen mask bears an exaggerated smile painted on it, so he always looks happy— and mostly he is, as his contagious laugh is recognizable. He has participated as a co-captain a couple of times, though his preference is the rough-and-tumble role of being a runner. As a rite of passage when he turned sixteen, through the guidance of his father and uncles, he joined the joy of running in the Mardi Gras.

At the end of a day of dashing after chickens, Rémy is covered in mud from head to toe from his antics through this unforgettable adventure. Except for work commitments, he never forgoes participating in the run, whether the weather is rainy, gloomy or sleeting. It took some practice and a few falls, but with bravado, Rémy has learned to steady himself and stand upright on a horse like a circus performer. The trick is balancing on the right kind of saddle. He loves to thrill spectators at his Mardi Gras—they call it "dancing on a horse" like a trick rider. Although he hasn't yet mastered doing a handstand while on a horse, it's on his bucket list for next year.

The Eunice Courir de Mardi Gras dates back to 1920. The courir was abandoned for a few years during World War II, but in 1946, a small band of riders revived the tradition.

On actual Mardi Gras day, the courir begins at 8:00 a.m. along a thirteen-mile route that visitors may follow. Participants ride in trailers or may ride on horseback. Many runners walk from farm to farm. They beg for gumbo ingredients like chickens or sausage. Financial donations are also welcomed. In exchange for generosity bestowed to them, the runners perform a dance. By midafternoon, they return to host a downtown parade and promenade with music and high-spirited fun.

Approximately two thousand people volunteer, so it's some big shindig that lasts from Friday through Tuesday. It kicks off on Friday before Mardi Gras, and each day, various events of live Cajun music and jam sessions are scheduled, as well as a dog parade, chasing of the chickens and parading of outrageous costumes.

The fun begins way before Tuesday! As part of the Mardi Gras celebration in Eunice, Lakeview Park & Beach hosts a community boucherie on Monday morning for Lundi Gras (Fat Monday) with offerings of cracklings, boudin, backbone stew and other pork dishes.

Mardi Gras is a huge cultural tradition in Louisiana but so is an old-fashioned boucherie (pig slaughter). Preparation for a wintertime boucherie began soon after the first cold snap appeared in southwest Louisiana. Leading up to the communal pig slaughter, pigs were penned and fattened by increasing the amount of grain in their diets. Many households in rural areas of our boot-shaped state did not have refrigeration until the 1960s or later.

The boucherie was certainly not a lavish affair. Rather, it was recognized as a necessity for feeding large families and also served as a way to prepare for upcoming holiday feasts. This dawn-to-dusk event became one big party for family and friends to sing, dance, play, joke, chase one another and work together to serve a daylong meal. Virtually every part of the pig, from the snout to the tail, was used to prepare a dish. Entrées included pork chops, ponce (pig stomach), boudin, cracklings, ham and hogshead cheese.

Lafourche Parish—Different Kind of Chase

Keep your eyes wide open when searching on the Louisiana map for the hamlets of Gheens (pronounced Gains); Chackbay, which has hosted the annual Louisiana Gumbo Festival for nearly fifty years; and Choupique (pronounced shoe pick), named in honor of the French term for bowfin fish/cypress trout. These Lafourche Parish villages embrace the Cajun French lifestyle through a rich history of sugarcane plantations, winding bayous and renowned fishing spots. And something else they have in common is that their version of the Mardi Gras dash is taken to a whole other, unexpected level of frivolity.

These unique Lafourche Parish communities have shared a love of their own style of Mardi Gras since the late 1800s. Their unusual approach can best be interpreted as a takeoff from another time, another world—but that's what makes it exciting. The antics here certainly don't resemble the New Orleans Carnival. And it's also vastly different from the Courir de Mardi Gras of Louisiana's prairie parishes. No one riding a horse and no chasing of chickens here! But chasing does indeed occur for the bizarre rituals.

Their Mardi Gras festivities begin with a morning parade in which anyone with a decorated vehicle, whether it be a convertible car, truck or wagon, can line up to roll through the heart of the community. And the float riders must have a stash of colorful beads or other tokens to toss to parade spectators. Following the chugging along of a cluster of floats and vehicles, a community gumbo is shared by all.

More than one hundred masked men in homemade costumes, some who resemble ghouls, prepare for this boisterous play with the intention of entertainment. And they chase children, not chickens. Part of the liberating roleplaying for this Mardi Gras is to encourage children to say their prayers. This event bears a similarity to medieval European flagellation rituals as the men reenact a reminder of the importance of praying, followed by lighthearted whipping of the children.

Elders of the tight-knit Lafourche Parish settlements are veterans of this sort of Mardi Gras, and they train and initiate the younger men, called "whippers" or "chasers." These elders symbolically pass the torch of this celebratory ritual to others. Care is taken in gathering the proper long willow switches. These will be used to lightly whip, not harm the kids. A set of tiny round bells is pinned to the whippers, who are dressed in colorful costumes and homemade scary masks. The Mardi Gras men, led by a captain, gather into trucks to begin a caravan through the neighborhoods. Once the quest is undertaken to find the kids, warnings are sounded. Horns are honked, and willow switches are tapped in a rhythmic beat on the side of the wagon. The men holler with glee as they search for willing children who have volunteered to participate in the ritual. And the chase is wild as the designated children try to outsmart the whippers by hiding under a house, trampling through ditches and searching for a secret spot to take cover. When children view the Mardi Gras coming toward them, they dash across the yards to hide in a mossy place as they attempt to escape masked men who are armed with switch in hand.

To express regret and penance for any bad behavior from the past year, the children learn to cry out "Pardon" so their flogging will be light—a tap on the child's back, arms or legs. If they do not express their regret, the whipping may be harsher. It's a symbol to show that their sins have been purged. Scary? You bet!

The majority of children have practiced their prayers the night before and are excited about the chasing and light flogging and are ready to recite The Lord's Prayer without stumbling. The show of atonement relates to the day after Mardi Gras, which is Ash Wednesday, thus beginning the somber Lenten season, in which many practice fasting and self-reflection.

TURKEY RUN

The Savoy family of the Eunice area play an integral role in preserving the Cajun ways through music and through Mardi Gras. A few years ago, they developed their own style of the Courir de Mardi Gras among friends, just outside of Eunice, with a run called Fiquetaïque (fack-ee-tie-yay), which means "turkey" in one of the Native American Indian languages. Keep it small and stay with traditions of the old days was the idea of this small community experience. Absolutely there are the crazy, one-of-a-kind costumes and sincere begging for gumbo ingredients, as well as lots of fun-loving misbehaving. Fiddles and accordions are on hand, and French is spoken by many participants and guests. The event rises to new heights by a challenge. Who can perform like Spiderman and crawl up the greased pole to rescue a caged guinea hen at the top? And the chase begins. On a more somber note, this group of revelers honors early Cajun fiddler Dennis McGee by making their final stop at McGee's gravestone to pray.

Mardi Gras Song

Cultures grow on the vine of tradition.
—Jonah Goldberg

Nothing gets a crowd a'going during Carnival more than the foot-stomping, exciting Mardi Gras song, which depicts the sequence of the quest of vagabond runners. The Mardi Gras who pursue the chickens in search of gumbo ingredients may chant lyrics in French. Slight variations in the various communities exist, though the tune is always high-energy. At each stop, when the song is played, runners become even more frenzied as the day goes on. They are captivated with the thrill of the chase, the entertainment, the French lyrics and the sharing of the somewhat unusual tradition under the direction of Le Capitaine. A gumbo at the end of the day is their goal.

The Cajun Mardi Gras song, either "La Danse de Mardi Gras" (The Mardi Gras Dance) or "La Vielle Chanson de Mardi Gras" (The Old Mardi Gras Song), is played on accordion, fiddle, triangle and guitar as the Mardi Gras runners travel from house to house.

The lyrics of the tale portray that the humble Mardi Gras runners do not want to be misunderstood as malefactors or evildoers. Simply, they are requesting permission to enter the farmer's homestead and beg for ingredients to cook a gumbo to feed their family. They are not asking for charity by collecting bags of rice or vegetables or *une patate* (a sweet potato) or even *une poule maigre* (a skinny chicken), which guarantees enough gumbo for everyone. In exchange for any collected ingredients, the runners will entertain by dancing and climbing on trees as they perform comedic antics.

One of the most popular and spirited performances of "La Danse de Mardi Gras" belongs to Steve Riley and the Mamou Playboys. The clip-clop of horses at the intro prepares you for the heartfelt story of Mardi Gras runners who, once a

Steve Riley is a renowned Cajun French musician known for his spirited rendition of "La Danse de Mardi Gras" with the Mamou Playboys. *Courtesy of St. Landry Parish Tourist Commission (info@cajuntravel.com).*

year, embrace traditions of the past and travel the countryside to play the role of someone else for a day as they collect items for a gumbo as their parents or grandparents did before them. They look to their leader, Le Capitaine, and await when he waves a flag for the runners to enter the homestead and begin to chant the Mardi Gras song.

Famed Cajun musician Steve Riley has played Cajun music with the Mamou Playboys for over thirty years. He recognizes that "La Danse de Mardi Gras" is one of the oldest songs of Cajun culture. Riley notes that the root of this song dates to the French celebration of Mardi Gras, before the Acadians migrated to Canada and then to Louisiana. "The prized song adds a contagious energy to the event."

Riley has many talents; not only is he a soulful songwriter and vocalist, but he also plays several instruments, such as the accordion, guitar and fiddle. At a young age, he experienced the excitement of being a Mardi Gras runner.

Surrounded by many talented musicians while growing up in Mamou, Riley was bitten by the Cajun music bug at a young age. "There were always a lot of musicians dropping in at my grandparents' house on the weekends," he shared. "My dad's family is from Eunice, so I would hear my cousin Marc Savoy play with Dennis McGee at house parties in Eunice. I heard Cyprien Landreneau at my parents' home in Mamou. I just grew up in the middle of it, and I always loved the music of the Balfa Brothers."

Riley accomplished many musical milestones at a young age. His grandfather Burke Guillory was a big influence early on by teaching Riley how to sing at age three. His Uncle Bobby coached him to play his first song on the accordion at age seven. At age thirteen, he had his own accordion. Being introduced to renowned Cajun musician Dewey Balfa at age fifteen led to touring with him. At age eighteen, Riley formed his own band, the Mamou Playboys.

"Mamou was one of the first towns to bring back the old traditional Mardi Gras," he said. "The people of my grandfather's generation were very involved in Cajun culture and its music. They were hanging out with the Balfa Brothers and Dennis McGee and were all instrumental in starting the Mamou Cajun Festival and bringing back the old traditional run."

Riley still gets a thrill performing in his hometown as thousands of people look on. He shared some reflections of growing up with the Mamou Mardi Gras. "Some of my best memories of playing music come from the iconic Holiday Lounge in Mamou. We performed from the Mardi Gras wagon that follows the run and ended up downtown in front of thousands of people."

Riley and his band released their first album in 1990, self-titled *Steve Riley and the Mamou Playboys*. It was produced by legendary Cajun musician Zachary Richard, who also lent backup vocals. The band's original version of "La Danse de Mardi Gras" appears on the album *La Toussaint* (1995). The newer version was released on the band's 2015 album *Voyageurs*.

A great honor in Riley's career was when his band performed "La Danse de Mardi Gras" for an episode during the second season of the HBO series *Treme*. Although the setting of this series is New Orleans, the scene of the Mardi Gras run actually represents western Louisiana. "The film crew came down a week after Mardi Gras, so we had to reenact and basically repeat an authentic Mardi Gras run," Riley said. "The stage was intense. The producers were nearby hanging out, and they said they wanted me to play the authentic Mardi Gras song at the next stop. They watched in awe as a chicken was thrown."

Riley concluded, "It has been a great life with amazing opportunities. It's been unbelievable that I have seen places that I probably wouldn't have visited otherwise. I've been so fortunate to be able to do what I love as I travel the world, play the music I love, and represent the culture that means so much to me."

Fiddler on the Run

Listen to the orchestra of sounds during the Mardi Gras run. Chickens squawk as they flee through terraced farmland. The runners breathe heavily as they climb to the farmhouse roof of an unsuspecting farmer. A pair of runners grunt as they fall in the mud and wallow around in it for fun. Titters of laughter rise from spectators delighted at the sight of runners falling. Ongoing whooping and hollering. A fiddle cries as it's being tuned by musician Luke Huval. Horses clip-clop in rhythm. Cows bellow in nearby fields, oblivious to the spectacle of their surroundings. Cheerful children jingle the coins in their pockets as they prepare to give up their change to the funny-looking Mardi Gras runners.

Overall, the musicians sing a rendition of upbeat songs as they ride in a wagon down a dusty road. The role of the musician during the Mardi Gras is to entertain and keep the runners elated—no matter if the sun is covered by clouds and it feels like the sky is falling.

Although musician Luke Huval is only in his early twenties, he has dressed in the traditional raggedy costume and belted out tunes with his

Luke Huval is a Cajun French musician. *Courtesy of Annette Huval.*

comrades for this Cajun ritual for seven years. His background is well rooted in the core of Cajun music. Luke has been influenced by many family members. His grandfather Percy picked up the accordion, a Falcon make, during his gray-haired years. He was a natural and formed an informal trio of Cajun musicians. Luke's mother, Annette, is a French teacher who has shared Cajun traditions through documentary oral storytelling. His father, Terry, and uncle Tony began playing instruments and performing in a Cajun band while in their teens. Luke was immersed in the French language through family ties and traveled through the French immersion program in Lafayette Parish; this exposure sparked a love of his heritage. At home, jam sessions were part of life with a piano, guitar, drums and fiddle on hand.

The first instrument he picked up was a guitar, then the accordion (he now has his grandfather's) and fiddle. He is also a talented vocalist, and singing French songs is second nature to him. He is a recipient of many accordion championships. He has led music camps for fiddle players as a way of sharing his love for music. As a college student majoring in civil engineering, he still devotes time to his passion of music. For two years, he joined a bluegrass ensemble, which exposed him to other beats and tunes. Through his interaction with fellow musicians, Luke has performed in the Lafayette area, including many festivals, beginning at age twelve. Opportunity has led him to play and sing at events such as the Natchitoches-NSU Folk Festival in Natchitoches. Outside of Louisiana, he has performed in Wisconsin; New York (along with the Cajun Hank Williams, musician D.L. Menard); southeast Texas; Raleigh, North Carolina (for a bluegrass festival); and New Brunswick, Canada. And the Grand Ole Opry in Nashville, Tennessee, welcomed Luke's fiddle playing in July 2022 as he, along with his father, musician Terry Huval, accompanied a Cajun musical legend, singer and songwriter Jo-El Sonnier. Luke regularly plays accordion with Zach Fuselier and fiddle with Dylan Aucoin.

There is no doubt that Luke prefers this kind of rural Mardi Gras, such as in Ossun, Louisiana, over the more formal parades and balls in larger cities. He recognizes that the runners are continually testing the captain. At each stop, Luke has performed the fast-paced Mardi Gras jig when the chicken is tossed up to the clouds in Ossun and Iota. The unexpected antics he views are memorable at the Best Stop Boudin shop with runners pretending to

Customers at a popular boudin spot are surprised by Mardi Gras runners. *Courtesy of Annette Huval.*

shoplift while customers are amazed when they are invited to dance to the Mardi Gras song. Following the Best Stop, a quick but much appreciated stop is made at a Mexican restaurant for margaritas, en route to a big bowl of gumbo for nourishment.

During his quiet time, Luke enjoys listening to a wide range of music but favors Cajun and country music. Check him out on Spotify.

Right: Many children in Louisiana prairie parishes are introduced to the joy of being a runner. *Courtesy of Roby Poché.*

Below: The runners must learn to sing the traditional Mardi Gras song in French. *Courtesy of Annette Huval.*

Left: Gumbo is a favored comfort dish in Louisiana. *Courtesy of St. Landry Parish Tourist Commission (info@cajuntravel.com).*

Below: The fun-loving marauders wear funny masks and raggedy costumes. *Courtesy of David Simpson and the St. Landry Parish Tourist Commission (info@cajuntravel.com).*

Dancing on a horse is one of the antics many "cowboy" runners perform. *Courtesy of Dwight Jodon and St. Landry Parish Tourist Commission (info@cajuntravel.com).*

Musicians keep the excitement going during the Courir de Mardi Gras. *Courtesy of Annette Huval.*

Top: King cake is celebrated during carnival time. *Courtesy of St. Landry Parish Tourist Commission (info@cajuntravel.com).*

Bottom: Many children embrace the traditions of the Tee Mamou run. *Courtesy of Annette Huval.*

The chicken chase is a thrill to watch. *Courtesy of Annette Huval.*

The Mermentau Cove Mardi Gras run begins early in the day, traveling through dusty roads to stop at welcoming farmhouses. *Courtesy of Annette Huval.*

The chicken chase is a thrill to watch. *Courtesy of Annette Huval.*

Any means of transportation is acceptable for this Mardi Gras runner. *Courtesy of Annette Huval.*

Le Capitaine takes his whip out to corral the runners. *Courtesy of Annette Huval.*

These chickens will not be used in a gumbo. *Courtesy of Annette Huval.*

There are many family-friendly crafts for Mardi Gras. *Courtesy of Annette Huval.*

These rascals love the rowdiness. *Courtesy of Annette Huval.*

Cinq sous (five cents) is what the beggar requests. *Courtesy of Annette Huval.*

Ready or not, jumping into a pond is part of the rites of passage. *Courtesy of Annette Huval.*

Steve Riley is a renowned Cajun French musician known for his spirited rendition of "La Danse de Mardi Gras" with the Mamou Playboys. *Courtesy of St. Landry Parish Tourist Commission (info@ cajuntravel.com).*

The town of Eunice celebrates the Cajun Mardi Gras annually from Friday to Tuesday with lots of music, food and celebrations. *Courtesy of St. Landry Parish Tourist Commission (info@ cajuntravel.com).*

Above: There are many free music jams throughout Cajun country. *Courtesy of David Simpson and St. Landry Parish Tourist Commission (info@cajuntravel.com).*

Left: A runner is tossed up in the air as everyone cheers. Hopefully, it will be a soft landing. *Courtesy of Annette Huval.*

Above: The Mermentau Cove Mardi Gras make a solemn stop at the historic Istre Cemetery to pay respects to the deceased, many of whom are family members. *Courtesy of Annette Huval.*

Left: Captain Devon Vincent cradles a chicken. *Courtesy of Annette Huval.*

Even riding a bike with flat tires can be fun for the Mardi Gras. *Courtesy of Annette Huval.*

Le Capitaine Chance Henry is responsible for keeping his runners in line while entertaining at a farmhouse during the Mermentau Cove Mardi Gras run. *Courtesy of Annette Huval.*

Brody Myers reins in his horse as he enjoys the Mardi Gras run. *Courtesy of Annette Huval.*

WHIMSICAL MARDI GRAS

THE ESSENTIALS

S trange, but true! Many parts to the colorful jigsaw puzzle of Mardi Gras seem quirky, all adding to the frivolity of the celebration. Also shared are important aspects of the Cajun culture.

Life is a masquerade. Everywhere you look are people hiding behind masks.
—Ridze Khan

ACADIAN FLAG—Some captains proudly carry the Acadian Flag to lead their runners and exemplify their legacy. Dr. Thomas J. Arceneaux designed the Louisiana Acadian Flag in 1965 in colors of red, white and blue to commemorate the two hundredth anniversary of the Acadian exile into Louisiana. Three silver fleurs-de-lis on the blue field represent the Acadians' French heritage, symbolizing the kings of France. A portion of the flag also represents Louisiana's Spanish heritage, as the "red field" bears a gold castle honoring Spain, the country that controlled Louisiana at the time of the Acadian migration. Acadiana's patron saint is the Virgin Mary, who is represented as the gold star on the flag's white field. In Louisiana, counties are called parishes. Acadiana has been defined as the twenty-two-parish area of southern Louisiana in which the majority of residents are Cajun or Creole. Lafayette is considered the heart of this region.

ARTISANS—Although the role they play is considered "behind the scenes," the creative efforts of artisans cannot be minimized. Hours are dedicated to designing and shaping expressive masks, capuchons (dunce hats), fringed

The screen wire mask is unique and a treasured keepsake. *Courtesy of Annette Huval.*

costumes, trophies and whips. These rustic getups derive from early rural costumes in France mocking the nobility, clergy and scholars. The variety of costumes varies, though basically they are sewn in a patchwork style with mixed colors and patterns. Since supplies were often limited in rural communities, homemakers became resourceful in finding fabric.

In the early 1800s, wooden barrels and large metal tins were used to transport and store grain, seed, animal feed and other staples. The downside of using barrels was that they were heavy and would sometimes leak. Metal tins would often rust, ruining the staple that they stored. Other means of storage, aside from barrels, specifically large feed sacks, were considered; lighter in weight though durable, they made transporting the containers from boats to docks to wagons to general stores less cumbersome. Feed sacks, originally of heavy canvas fabric, were improved when industrial sewing machines capable of sewing double locking seams were invented. This ensured that the sacks would not burst open during transportation. During the late 1800s, the fabric was switched to an inexpensive cotton. These early feed sacks bore the logos of products such as flour, sugar, animal feed, seeds, rice and fertilizer.

To make costumes, many homemakers had used old shirts, though they gladly incorporated the new source by looking at the fabric of the flour feed sacks to create costumes. The sizes of the feed sacks varied, and a variety of pleasing, somewhat colorful prints were produced. This made the feed sacks especially useful for resourceful homemakers who used their sewing prowess to cut up the sacks to sew pillowcases, children's clothes and undergarments. And it further served as a frugal means for making Mardi Gras costumes.

Wire screen masks for Mardi Gras, now largely handcrafted locally, were once mass-produced. Beginning in the late 1800s, the masks were imported and sold in southwestern Louisiana. The unusual wire screen masks were largely made in China and the Caribbean.

BABY DOLLS—A famous red-light district of pleasure houses in New Orleans at the beginning of the twentieth century, Storyville, had two sections—one for white patrons and one for Black. In 1912, a group of African American women planned on dressing up for Mardi Gras. To exaggerate their innocence, they wore short pleated skirts, silk bloomers and little hair bonnets, and some carried baby bottles. Calling themselves the Baby Dolls, the women boldly exaggerated their demure appearance by heavily powdering and rouging their faces. They are considered the first organization for parading women and continue to draw attention to their innocence on Mardi Gras.

BEADS, BAUBLES AND DOUBLOONS—Many rural communities with simpler parades throw plastic bead necklaces and miniature Tootsie Roll candies to eager crowds. As floats stream by, crowds of die-hard fans set up a stepladder so they may more easily reach to catch the best souvenirs tossed from the float riders. Many yell "Throw me something, mister" or try to get attention in hopes of getting the prizes. Many krewes go all out and are very creative. In New Orleans, Zulu throws coconuts; Muses throws shoes; Nyx throws purses; and the Krewe of Carrollton throws decorated shrimp boots, which often come in handy in Louisiana.

Tossing trinkets for parades became a tradition in New Orleans in the mid-1800s, providing a valued keepsake to make the experience memorable. Many krewes in elaborate parades throw bundles of doubloons, plastic cups, toys and other souvenirs. Commemorative dated aluminum doubloons—which resemble coins—were introduced to Mardi Gras in New Orleans in 1960. Doubloons from early parades are now considered collectibles. Most float riders of the Cajun Mardi Gras parades or promenades do not toss out trinkets, preferring to keep le bon vieux temps (the good old days) of an earlier time.

BIRTHPLACE OF AMERICA'S MARDI GRAS—Mobile, Alabama, has French ties dating to 1702 and is considered America's birthplace of Mardi Gras. The "Azalea City" of Mobile continues to celebrate Carnival season southern style, complete with parades, masking and elaborate balls. A favorite throw at Mobile parades is the Moon Pie, a tasty, hand-sized, chocolate-covered marshmallow pie.

CAJUN FRENCH LANGUAGE—PARLEZ-VOUS? It's another aspect of the Cajun culture that is so important, as many champion the cause for preserving the use of the French language. Through the Courir de Mardi Gras, many participants have learned chants, jokes and lyrics as they embrace conversational Cajun French. Musicians have also learned the language to interject into their Cajun or zydeco music.

At one time, however, a stigma was attached to speaking Cajun French in Louisiana, and the use of it was often suppressed. Speaking French was considered a symbol of "backward" country folk, so many stopped using the language. Many children from the 1920s to the 1950s grew up speaking only the French of their parents. Often, they were limited in their reading, writing or English skills. This certainly presented a dilemma when they had to begin school. In the classroom, they were chastised for speaking French and may have been punished by various means. How many children had to write multiple lines, "I will not speak French," or were punished by kneeling on raw rice if the teacher overheard French phrases? This attitude caused a major loss of passing the ancestral language on to future generations in Louisiana.

Luckily the French of our ancestors can still be heard at grocery stores, gas stations, restaurants, festivals and community events. Many children strived to learn French, as they were keen to interpret what their grandparents were talking about. Their ears perked up with MawMaw saying something about *gateau* (cake) or PawPaw suggesting *pecher* (fishing). Usually, the first expression the kids recognized in French was *"l'école est fermée"* for "School is closed."

Since the importance of maintaining Cajun French has been acknowledged, many efforts have been created to preserve the language. The Council for the Development of French in Louisiana (CODOFIL) was established in 1968 to help revitalize interest in the French language, tying into the educational system. CODOFIL continues to play a key role in preserving Louisiana's French roots by providing scholarships for the study of French abroad as well as funding multimedia productions developed, created and distributed by French-speaking Louisiana citizens. The initiative also supports French teachers in Louisiana schools and organizes special events highlighting the French language. The organization has promoted French immersion programs that introduce children in first grade all the way to twelfth grade to incorporating Cajun French as part of their daily education. Today, approximately twenty-six French immersion schools exist in eight Louisiana parishes. Some schools allow their older students to visit nursing homes to reconnect to their heritage by interacting with the residents who speak French.

A cultural organization in Arnaudville named NUNU hosts French tables in which participants can meet regularly. No formal agenda exists; it's simply an event to listen and speak in Cajun French. NUNU also sponsors cooking classes, potluck suppers, art exhibits and music events as a valuable means to preserve the Cajun culture.

The Cajun French Music Association (CFMA) promotes and preserves the Cajun French culture, through Cajun fiddle and accordion lessons, jam sessions and dancing lessons. Founded in 1984, the CFMA has seven chapters in Louisiana and three chapters in southeast Texas.

Cajuns—Descendants of the Acadians, refugees from France, who settled in Acadie, a key location in the maritime region of Canada. The majority of these first settlers of what is now known as Nova Scotia were considered peasants or farmers who were Catholic and family-oriented and remain so for the most part. Exiled by the British who took over Nova Scotia, the Acadians experienced a massive deportation, and many ended up in southwest Louisiana during the mid-1700s.

The Captain, or Le Capitaine—Directs the rural community Courir de Mardi Gras as he rides on horseback. He is the leader, and though unmasked, he wears a cowboy hat and an elaborate cloak in the Mardi Gras colors of purple, green and gold. He keeps the runners in line, which is a big responsibility, as many runners may have enjoyed a variety of alcoholic refreshments. At each stop, the lead captain approaches the homeowner at their farm and asks for permission to come into the yard, allowing the runners to perform. Once the homeowner accepts the invitation, the captain waves a flag. The runners, first those on horseback followed by those crowded on wagons, invade the homestead. He keeps score of who catches the chicken at each stop, as rustic awards are given for many categories. Le Capitaine encourages suspending reality just for the day. Forget about "breaking news" and flat tires and enjoy the activities. As he barks orders to keep everyone in line, he holds a whip in one hand, which he has no hesitation to use, and a white flag in the other.

Carnival—The word stems from the Latin *carne vale*, which means "farewell to meat," as many Catholics abstain from eating meat on Fridays during the Lenten season.

The Chicken—Plays an integral role at each stop during the runs. The brave fowl is thrown precariously in the air, and the chase begins amid a flurry of feathers as it darts trying to escape. The fat hen will be tired out by end of day and will not actually be thrown into the gumbo pot, nor will it be hurt or smashed by the runners. *Le poulet* (the chicken) has played memorable roles in Louisiana as a main ingredient in gumbo as well as providing humorous entertainment during the chicken chase at the Mardi Gras. Fowl, specifically roosters, served as contenders during past

Left: Captain Devon Vincent cradles a chicken. *Courtesy of Annette Huval.*

Below: That chicken is fast! *Courtesy of Annette Huval.*

years in cockfighting battles. The blood sport dates to ancient Persia and was introduced in North America in the late 1700s. Many in Louisiana considered this brave barnyard bird tradition as social entertainment, and gambling was part of the attraction. An iconic roadhouse in Acadiana, Jay's in Cankton, hosted lively music and dancing as well as regularly scheduled cockfighting matches. So popular and unusual was this phenomenon that some patrons on the dancefloor held their rooster even though the contenders were equipped with razors on their spurs. It has not been documented, however, if the gamecocks preferred the waltz or the Cajun jig before they entered into the fight at the on-site ring. With dollar bills in hand, attendees circled around the fighting pit as they encouraged their favorite contender in the gruesome competition in a flurry of feathers. Louisiana was the last U.S. state to ban cockfighting, in 2007.

COLORS OF MARDI GRAS—Traditional colors of purple, which stands for justice; green, which represents faith; and gold, which represents power.

CREOLES—The definition of Creoles has been modified through the years. At one time, it referred to people of European heritage born in colonial Louisiana during French or Spanish rule. Then, the meaning was extended to include African heritage as well. *Creoles of Color* is a term often designated to mean mixed heritage. Cajun and Creole cooking have many similarities.

DRINKING IN THE STREETS—Take heed of advice that if you plan to treat yourself to an alcoholic beverage during Mardi Gras, it is wise to check local ordinances. In some communities, both big and small, it is acceptable to drink on the streets during festival time, though usually not from a glass container. Public drunkenness is not acceptable, nor is driving a vehicle while tipsy or intoxicated.

EPIPHANY—Christian feast day of January 6, which celebrates the three wise men's visit to the baby Jesus. This day is considered the official start of carnival season.

FLAMBEAUX—from the French word *flambe*, meaning "flame." Electric lighting was not available during the eighteenth century. Partygoers wanted to view the elaborate displays of Mardi Gras, so organizers began using gas light torches known as flambeaux to illuminate the procession of brightly decorated carriages. The lights were considered to "light the way to lent." The Mistick Krewe of Comus in New Orleans was the first group to incorporate the French customs of flambeaux. In 1857, they debuted a parade with lighting to better enhance their costumes and procession, using the theme of Milton's *Paradise Lost*.

Above: Comus Ball. *Courtesy of LSU Museum of Art, Caroline Wogan Durieux Collection.*

Opposite: Rex, King of the Carnival. *Courtesy of LSU Museum of Art, Caroline Wogan Durieux Collection.*

GIANT BULL—The famous Rex parade in New Orleans is led by an iconic papier mâché sculpture of a giant bull's head. The fattened bull, *Boeuf Gras*, is a symbol taken from the Butchers' Guild of Paris, which began the tradition of leading a fattened bull symbolizing the last feast for citizens to savor before Lent began. For a time in medieval France, a live bull was adorned with a garland of roses around its neck, its horns and hooves gilded, and draped in white as it was paraded straight from the stockyards through the streets. However, in Louisiana, many Catholics who observe Lent may skip steaks and pork chops on Fridays but partake of fruits of the sea instead. It has been documented that in 1805, Napoleon I supported the custom of the Fat Bull Fete, which took place on Sunday, Monday and Shrove Tuesday, to draw visitors to Paris. However, the festive procession of the live bull ended with its sacrifice. A romantic participant of the showy parade was a small child with golden locks dressed as Cupid.

KREWES—These social clubs host Mardi Gras balls and may participate in parades by sponsoring a float. One of the oldest and best-known krewes in New Orleans is Rex, since 1872, which held the first daytime parade.

LUNDI GRAS—Fat Monday is the day before Fat Tuesday/Mardi Gras. In many communities, celebrations are also held on this day to extend carnival festivities, as this is the time to "Eat, Drink and Be Merry."

MARDI GRAS BOAT PARADES—You can cruise on the water for a special Mardi Gras parade if you have a navigable waterway, and Louisiana has plenty. In 1973, in the quaint town of Madisonville, the Krewe of Tchefuncte launched an event to tie Mardi Gras with love for their river. The boat parade is typically held on a Saturday two weeks before Mardi Gras.

MARDI GRAS CELEBRATIONS AT THE HANSEN'S DISEASE CENTER—In 1894, an abandoned sugarcane plantation in Iberville Parish named Indian Camp became the site of the first U.S. facility dedicated to the quarantine of those infected with Hansen's disease, once known as leprosy. It was known as the Louisiana Leper Home and later became a medical facility. Located between Baton Rouge and New Orleans, the site accepted patients from throughout the U.S. Despite extreme hardships and dire circumstances of the patients, many tried to incorporate a sense of normal life by socializing with one another and hosting seasonal events. This included Mardi Gras celebrations in which residents wore masks and costumes and organized parades within the grounds. Miniature floats were fashioned from bicycles, carts and patients riding in wheelchairs. Tongue in cheek, the Mardi Gras Krewe of Carville even honored a king and queen each year at the formal ball. As throws, collectible aluminum doubloons were imprinted with the outline of an armadillo, an animal that was believed to carry the bacterial infection that causes Hansen's disease. The medical facility and research center was closed in 1999 and now serves as a museum and an adjoining cemetery that can be visited.

MARDI GRAS INDIANS—In groups, Black men have dressed as Indians during Carnival season for more than fifty years as a focus on African heritage. Their costumes are celebrated, as this illustrious group proudly flaunts its showpieces. Their regalia is made of a wide range of rich materials such as satin, fur, velvet and metallic cloth. Rhinestones, imitation pearls and embroidery adornment of intricate design are used to further glamorize the getups. From a headdress of ostrich plumes, which symbolize flight and freedom, to the dazzling beaded moccasins, the Indians are attired to draw attention. Creation of this krewe is believed to have roots in the appearance of groups of Plains Indians who traveled to the South to perform in Wild West shows highlighting horses and wagons. This is further associated with Buffalo Bill's Wild West Show, which wintered in New Orleans in 1884–85.

MARDI GRAS MUSICIANS AND THEIR MAGICAL INSTRUMENTS—The music makers dress in raggedy costumes and wear fanciful masks in the same fashion as runners. They ride the Mardi Gras wagon, and at each stop they perform music by cranking up the accordion, plucking the fiddle and tinging the triangle as the vocalists belt out songs. Through their efforts of singing and dancing, spectators are enticed to join in. During the day, the bravado of the runners increases with a mix of fellowship and liquid courage.

PARADE LADDERS—The parade route of a big Mardi Gras parade is often lined with colorfully decorated ladders. It serves a purpose more than decoration, as it allows children to climb up the rungs so they may see the festivities. Also, it gives an edge to being closer to the floats to catch the prized throws.

PARDONING OF THE CRAWFISH—At Thanksgiving, beginning with President Abraham Lincoln's time in office, the White House has unofficially pardoned a turkey from being roasted for the family gathering. The first family had received a turkey as a gift, and Lincoln's son adopted the fowl as a

Popular Cajun Instruments

ACCORDION—Often called a squeezebox, first made in Germany in the 1820s. It was likely introduced by German immigrants who traveled to South Louisiana with this versatile musical instrument in hand. The Cajun French musical genre became popularized in 1928 through Joseph Falcon and his future wife, Cleoma Breaux, considered the pioneering rock stars of Cajun music. Columbia Records of New Orleans recorded the duo's two songs, both sung in French: the two-step "Lafayette," also called "Allons a Lafayette," and recorded on the B side of "The Waltz That Carried Me to My Grave," or "La Valse Qui m'a Porter a Ma Tombe." Falcon played a button accordion, and Cleoma played a guitar. This also began the Cajun music and dancing craze at dancehalls. A year later, Creole musician Amede Ardoin, who often carried his prized accordion in a flour sack, and Cajun fiddler Dennis McGee recorded six songs together. This was groundbreaking for the times, because of the racially integrated collaboration. This led to further popularization of the accordion in Louisiana, especially in the prairie parishes, as several renowned artisans began making accordions.

FIDDLE OR VIOLIN—The mainstay musical instrument used in Canada by Acadians prior to the mid-1700s expulsion. Many cultures have plucked the fiddle to the tunes of bluegrass to country to classical to Cajun and zydeco music.

TRIANGLE (T-FER)—Also called a "ting-a-ling," the triangle is a simple percussive rhythm instrument made of metal, often forged. There are two parts: the actual triangle, and the baton or beater, which is used to strike it. The nickname *t-fer* is a derivative of the French phrase *petit fer* for "little iron." It's an essential for keeping time to musical performances, especially for the accordion player.

RUBBOARD—Corrugated metal is what makes the "changa-changa" sound when this musical instrument is rubbed, especially while zydeco music is performed. It adds to the flavor of a lively tempo and is also known as a *frottoir* in French, meaning "scrubbing." The rubboard may have derived from recycled metal trays found in old-time refrigerators, though eventually laundry washboards were adapted to customize this rustic musical instrument. A variety of tools may be used as a "scratcher," such as thimbles, spoons, quarters or specialized gloves with rivets attached.

Mardi Gras Songs

The iconic "Mardi Gras Mambo," which declares that "it takes a cool cat to blow a horn," was written in 1953 and recorded one year later as a country song. "Iko Iko" was written during the early 1950s and later recorded by a New Orleans girls group called the Dixie Cups. The lyrics derive from a blend of Mardi Gras Indian chants as two of the tribes faced each other before they clashed. The song "Hey Pocky-Way" derives from New Orleans street chanting. The song has been recorded by many musicians, including the Grateful Dead. "Take Me to the Mardi Gras" was written by Paul Simon and recorded in 1975. The lyrics refer to the spiritually cleansing experience of New Orleans where you can "lay your burdens down" and "let the music wash your soul." Another rousing song, which is recognizable by the added element of whistling, is "Go to the Mardi Gras," co-written and recorded by Professor Longhair. The song urges everyone, "You ought to go see the Mardi Gras." It was also later recorded by Fats Domino.

Mystick Krewe of Louisianians

The spirit of Louisiana is felt in Washington, D.C., when Mardi Gras celebrations are spearheaded by the Mystick Krewe. The idea for celebrating began in 1944. The first ball featured statesman Hale Boggs dressed as George Washington. To add to the glamour, Louisiana festival queens from small communities were invited to attend the krewe ball. In 1953, CBS news commentator Walter Cronkite served as narrator of the growing event, and Vice President Richard Nixon presented the carnival queen. In 1981, after a long history of being involved in carnival festivities, the Mystick Krewe of Louisianians was incorporated as a nonprofit, official sponsor of the ball. What began as a way to share the spirit of Mardi Gras with all of America grew into a means to showcase many of Louisiana's tourism treasures. Louisiana music and samples of food continue to entice visitors as representatives of the Bayou State toss unique throws and host a formal masquerade ball. The celebration attracts two thousand revelers each year, while many newcomers to Cajun culture are delighted by their introduction to gumbo, grits and king cake.

Other Countries Where Mardi Gras Is Celebrated

BRAZIL—One of the most famous carnivals takes place in Rio de Janeiro, Brazil. The gala includes a promenade of over-the-top costumes and a samba dance parade led by King Momo, the ancient Greek god of mockery.

CANADA—Drawing on its French roots, Quebec, Canada, has celebrated its own style of Mardi Gras since the late 1800s. Reigning over the worship of snow and ice, a party king known as Bonhomme is the official representative of the Quebec Winter Carnival. The lovable snowman made his first appearance in 1955 and embodies the joie de vivre of the area. The festival is complete with ice sculpture competitions, dog sledding and lots of partying.

CROATIA—Located in the northwestern part of the Balkan Peninsula, the country of Croatia bears a Mediterranean flair and is blessed with a coastline of one thousand islands. The Rijeka (meaning "river") Carnival draws thousands of thrill seekers annually. Partying, masking and parades are part of the fun for celebrating before the start of the

Lenten season. Beloved traditions are celebrated, including chasing away wintertime's evil spirits in preparation for a brighter future. To accomplish this colorful feat, a troupe of one hundred bell ringers, the Zvončari, dress in sheepskins and wear exaggerated horned animal masks, cattle skulls or tall hats as they roam the streets. They swagger about carrying wooden clubs, and tied around their waists are huge, heavy cowbells that sound out loudly.

FRANCE—The city of Nice's wildly celebrated carnival along the French Riviera dates to a pagan festival from AD 1200 that was called Carne Levare (remove the flesh). Through the years, Nice incorporated other activities such as a flower parade to showcase regional flora and represent upcoming blossoms of springtime.

GREECE—The carnival of Patras, Greece, begins on January 17 (St. Anthony Day) and includes balls, parades, a hidden treasure hunt and a children's carnival, all ending with a ritual burning of the carnival king at the St. Nikolaos Street pier in the harbor of Patras. Aside from much frivolity, this ancient carnival was held to chase away the cold of winter leading to welcoming in springtime. Part of the celebration includes Burnt Thursday, a special day dedicated to the grilling of meats by partygoers before Lent begins.

TRINIDAD—Considered a sunny, rum-soaked celebration, Trinidad's Port of Spain Carnival parade began when human enslavement was ending. This warranted newly freed citizens to mimic their former French aristocratic owners, thus beginning a celebration of freedom. It is believed the first modern Caribbean Carnival celebrated in Trinidad occurred in the late eighteenth century when an influx of French settlers came to Trinidad, bringing with them one of their favorite traditions. The parades and bejeweled cultural costumes are famous in this part of the world. An integral slice of the celebration are the steelpan bands, which feature African percussion music.

pet. An animal lover himself, President Lincoln decided to spare the turkey's life. Louisiana has its own twist on lending mercy by pardoning its iconic crawfish on the first Tuesday after Mardi Gras as a way to kick off the official start of crawfish season. The Bayou State is a top producer of crawfish; many embrace the crustacean, which can be prepared boiled, fried or in an étouffée. Beginning in 2017, under Louisiana lieutenant governor Billy Nungesser, the life of a crawfish has been saved and an official proclamation issued. The likes of crawfish tagged as Clyde, Emile and Lafitte have heroically been averted from the boiling pot, treated like royalty and released in a waterway to swim away freely.

What a celebration—I captured a chicken! *Courtesy of Dwight Jodon and St. Landry Parish Tourist Commission.*

THE RUNNERS—Band of masked runners, may also be called collectively "The Mardi Gras," that performs a variety of unexpected and humorous antics. Consider them actors who enthusiastically engage in spoofs of carousing spontaneously, depending on which props they come across. Once permission is granted to enter the designated Mardi Gras stop, the runners on horseback charge at full speed, followed by the wagons filled with additional excited runners who remain ready to perform. The runners pour out of the wagon, which houses newbies as well as experienced masqueraders. Placed on another wagon is an ice chest and a port-o-let, both of which are very important. Often, a cage of chickens to be "chased" has been gathered by the krewe, as not all stops actually raise chickens. The runners get a kick out of disguising their voices so as not to be recognizable. Strict rules to follow have been formed regarding use of foul language, consumption of alcohol and knowing the Mardi Gras chant in French.

THROW ME A COCONUT, MISTER—The Zulu Social Aid and Pleasure Club is one of the oldest African American krewes in New Orleans, beginning in the early 1900s. Original costumes included African warrior wear of long black underwear, grass skirts and wooly wigs. Faces were blackened, and for emphasis the eyes and mouths were circled with white face paint. One of the most important roles was of the Royal Witch Doctor, who wore a horned headdress and gold ring in his nose. A creative alternative to throwing beads to parade fans was devised. When someone reaches out to catch a prized throw, the reward is a coconut, rather than beads (who would have guessed?). Rather than purchasing expensive glass beads, which was the common material of earlier beads, Zulu ventured to fruit stands in the French Market to purchase actual hairy coconuts. Gradually, the coconuts, sometimes tagged as a "Golden Nugget," are now shaved down and made lighter by a modification of draining out the milk and meat. The coconuts are decorated to resemble golden football helmets reminiscent of uniforms of the New Orleans Saints football team or creatively painted and sprinkled with glitter. To prevent accidents occurring when visitors could easily be knocked out by a tossed coconut, the throws are gently handed out. The early krewe king wore a lard can for a crown and carried a banana stalk for a scepter. In 1949, master trumpeter Louis Armstrong fulfilled a lifetime dream. Not only did the New Orleans native reign as king of jazz, but he also served as the king of Zulu to lead the parade.

WHEN AND WHERE WAS THE FIRST MARDI GRAS IN NORTH AMERICA? A rivalry exists of which city hosts the biggest, the best and the first. Where was the first Mardi Gras celebrated in North America? Historians believe

Specialties for Sampling during Mardi Gras

BLUE BELL CREAMERY makes a delightful Mardi Gras King Cake Ice Cream that promises a colorful cream cheese swirl with fairy bits of crunchy candy sprinkles of purple, gold and green. Scoop up cinnamon and vanilla flavors.

ABITA BREWING COMPANY of St. Tammany Parish, Louisiana, brews a seasonal, full-bodied, light amber beer. Mardi Gras Bock has pilsner and caramel malts and German Perle hops. Pour into a cold mug and enjoy the crisp taste. If you prefer a lightly carbonated soda, they also celebrate Carnival season with a King Cake Soda featuring the sweetness of frosting, candied sugar and cinnamon. It's made with pure Louisiana cane sugar and artesian spring water and is caffeine-free.

NOLA BREWERY of New Orleans brews a seasonal Belgian pale ale with a hint of citrus called Muses, named after a well-known all-female Mardi Gras krewe of the Big Easy.

COMMUNITY COFFEE loves Carnival time with its Mardi Gras King Cake Coffee of cinnamon and vanilla hints. Along the bayous, drinking strong Louisiana coffee remains part of life. *La gregue est chaude* is a common, neighborly front porch expression meaning "the coffeepot is hot" in French.

BAYOU TECHE BREWERY of Arnaudville says *A votre santé* (to your health) with its seasonal artisan version of a French farmhouse-style ale called Courir de Mardi Gras. It's brewed with pilsner, wheat and Munich malt and Saaz hops.

GAMBINO'S KING CAKE RUM CREAM is made with aged Caribbean rum, Wisconsin cream and Louisiana sugarcane. For over seventy years, Gambino's Bakery has been one of the top spots in New Orleans for delicious baked goods, including its hallmark King Cake. Now, a delicious rum cream is available to add something special for unique cocktails or prepared as a base for warmed-up rum sauce topping over bread pudding.

that it was celebrated in Fort Louis de la Louisiane, now known as Mobile, Alabama, in the early 1700s. However, a simpler celebration was held four years earlier through French-Canadian explorer Pierre Le Moyne d'Iberville Sieur de Bienville, who led an expedition to explore the coastline of the Mississippi Sound. During the scouting of the area, the team traveled through longboats to locate the mouth of the river sixty miles due south of New Orleans and dubbed the campsite Pointe du Mardi Gras. In true French fashion, as Mardi Gras was a popular time for partying, the men had thoughts of their families, who were likely in the midst of celebrations across the sea. The timing was right for the group to host an impromptu party (though no parade) on Fat Tuesday, 1699.

WHEN IS MARDI GRAS? Since the late sixteenth century, Mardi Gras, Fat Tuesday, Shrove Tuesday or Carnival Day has occurred on a Tuesday and is followed by Ash Wednesday, which begins the Christian season of Lent. Is Mardi Gras ever on Valentine's Day—February 14? Yes, this makes the celebration a memorable mix of Cupid's bow while you throw in a mix of green, gold and purple décor. And how is the date of Mardi Gras and Easter determined? Easter occurs on the first Sunday after the paschal full moon, or first full moon after March 21. Mardi Gras is a moveable holiday and falls forty-seven days before Easter Sunday. In 1875, Louisiana's Governor Henry Warmouth signed the Mardi Gras Act declaring that Fat Tuesday is a legal holiday in the Bayou State.

WE CALL IT MARDI GRAS. Many fun-loving events where life is temporarily "flipped," similar to Mardi Gras, have thrived in other cultures. Mardi Gras is also known as Shrove Tuesday, derived from the word *shrive*, which means "to give absolution after hearing confession." Many Catholics confess their sins in preparation for Lent, which begins on Ash Wednesday, the day after Shrove Tuesday.

PANCAKE DAY is another celebration that bears similarity to the Louisiana Mardi Gras. This is the day to enjoy a final rich treat of a pancake or sweeter crepe made from a filling batter of milk, butter, sugar, eggs and flour as a last indulgence before the beginning of Lent.

FASCHING is a five-day celebration based on medieval customs, primarily celebrated in German-speaking countries, and includes revelry through costumed parades and masked balls. Townspeople wear frightening wooden masks, many with demonic horns and bulging warts. This drives out evil spirits that have settled in the region over the cold, dreary winter. Once the spirits have been ousted, sunshine and gentler weather greet the townspeople once again, causing healthy crops to reappear. The first day of Fasching is dedicated to the women who routinely play jokes as they walk through town, including snipping the bottom of men's neckties.

WASSAILING involves merrymakers visiting from house to house for Christmas caroling as they raise their glasses to toast good health to their neighbors. Wassailing has been celebrated in the United Kingdom for centuries and is rooted in a pagan custom where country folks sang to fruiting trees and spirits in hopes of welcoming an abundant harvest. It generally takes place on Twelfth Night.

MUMMING involves play-acting where men and women swap clothes and mask up as they spread joy by singing and dancing for their neighbors. It is primarily celebrated in the United Kingdom. It occurs around the winter solstice to represent the cycle of death and resurrection.

THE FEAST OF FOOLS originated as a religious event throughout England and France honoring the Feast of the Circumcision, which supposedly took place on January 1. It transitioned, tongue in cheek, as an event to allow the church's lower-ranking clergy to poke fun at higher authority through role reversal in which peasants became kings for a day. Christian morals were replaced with rampant acts of wild behavior, presided over by a child who was appointed as Bishop of Fools. References to this feast are made in Victor Hugo's novel *The Hunchback of Notre Dame*, in which the main character, Quasimodo, is crowned Pope of Fools.

JAMBALAYA, CRAWFISH PIE, FILÉ GUMBO

Most seasonings are based on family tradition
—Master chef Wolfgang Puck

Take a look at the big picture, as the word *gumbo* has a far-reaching meaning beyond our cherished, rustic dish served year-round in Louisiana. The one-pot delight cooking on the stove filled with chunks of chicken and sausage represents the Cajun culture. As an artistic metaphor, it has been said that the state of Louisiana is truly a gumbo, or eclectic mix, of cultures, meaning Creoles, Cajuns, Italians, Germans, Native Americans, Africans, Spanish, French and others. The culinary shining star of gumbo draws from the cross-cultural melding of foodways. Although October 12 is considered National Gumbo Day, we like to celebrate it lackadaisically. Anytime we're hungry for some comfort food, no matter the season or the weather, it is time to pull out the gumbo bowls and spoons. Gumbo is considered an economical dish because it can feed a group of people. Patience must be practiced, as experienced cooks admit that the best gumbos simmer on the stove all day long.

Food historians proclaim that our amazing mélange of gumbo, originally considered a peasant dish, evolved from the French stew *pot-au-feu*, which means "pot on fire." There are recipes, once called receipts, from which this favored variation of our dish of gumbo was created before Louisiana became a state in 1812.

Cutting onions in preparation for cooking a gumbo. *Courtesy of St. Landry Parish Tourist commission (info@cajuntravel.com).*

This rich delight we crave as comfort food is a thick, hearty soup. It's so popular that it has been designated as our state's official cuisine and can be served as a cup-sized appetizer or in a meal-sized big bowl. It seems to soothe your soul and warm your heart. For many, the whiffs of the trinity vegetables sautéing and roux simmering on the stove often draw up memories of childhood from MawMaw's kitchen. Cooked for hours using seafood or meat, the gumbo's countless spices are perked up with layers of flavor. Pairings include shrimp and okra, duck and andouille, crabmeat and shrimp with a few oysters for a smoky taste, as well as chicken and sausage in which a chunk of tasso is added for a rich flavor.

To add extra protein to a gumbo, some cooks drop in a peeled hardboiled egg. Endless variations of gumbo are enjoyed by cooks; most gumbo, however, is served over fluffy rice. For health reasons, some households serve gumbo over cauliflower rice. Ah, the virtues of gumbo! When a host proclaims, "I'm making a gumbo," it usually means preparing bowls of gumbo accompanied by side dishes and visiting with lots of friends and family. It quickly turns into a social gathering.

The word *gumbo* derives from an African word for okra (*gombo*). How did okra come to the New World? It has been traced to the Transatlantic slave trade in the 1700s, when slaves were brought to the Americas. Many enslaved African women braided okra seeds into their hair to bring something easily planted to the new country. They could also transport something familiar from their homeland.

In today's modern kitchen, once your workspace is scattered with proper ingredients of a wooden spoon and the right stockpot for cooking a gumbo, let a glass of wine or a cold mug of beer keep you company as your stir the roux. Spoiler alert—some cooks purposely set aside two cans of their favorite beer when prepping ingredients to cook a gumbo. One can is poured into the gumbo pot during the stirring of the roux. The beer serves as their "secret ingredient" to enhance the taste. The second can of beer is obviously dedicated for the enjoyment of the cook. Each step of the process of making a gumbo on the stove has a wonderful aroma.

Some essentials of a simmering pot of gumbo include the following:

ANDOUILLE (ahn-doo-eee). Pork sausage that is heavily spiced and smoked. It's a popular ingredient to add in Cajun cuisine such as gumbo and jambalaya.

BAY LEAF originates from the evergreen bay laurel tree from the Mediterranean region. Throw a leaf or two into any simmering soup and especially in gumbo. It adds a slightly menthol taste to your prized dish. Once the gumbo is ready to be served, take care to pull out your bay leaves.

CAJUN OR CREOLE GUMBO. The basic ingredients differ, though preparation techniques are similar. For both styles, you begin with the trinity of vegetables and a roux. Cajun roux consists of flour and oil, while Creole roux combines flour and butter. In some recipes, tomatoes may be a key ingredient in Creole gumbo. A popular expression says that a Creole gumbo feeds one family with three chickens. However, a Cajun gumbo stretches the dish further by feeding three families with only one chicken.

CAYENNE PEPPER. This pantry staple packs a punch of heat in Louisiana. Also tagged as "red pepper," it is used liberally in its powdered form for cooking many Cajun dishes. The popular pepper originated in Cayenne, French Guyana.

COOKING TOOL BASICS. A sizable cast-iron pot, stockpot or a Dutch oven is suitable because usually when you're planning to cook a gumbo, you can't cook just a "little bit" of gumbo. A long wooden spoon for stirring the roux helps prevent burning and scratching your cookware. For scooping and serving your gumbo, a ladle will work. If you cook rice often, having a rice cooker is a good idea.

COWBOY CAVIAR. A black-eyed pea and tomato salad with a vinegary dressing. In the Deep South, these legumes are served in one form or another for New Year's Day. To guarantee good luck for what's coming up for our future into the new year, we enjoyed a spoonful or two of black-eyed peas and shredded cabbage coleslaw. The black-eyed pea, also known as "cowpeas," originated in Africa and is a good source of protein. These "magical" peas represent coins, and the greens of cabbage represent dollar currency, forecasting a future of good financial fortune.

FILÉ (pronounced "fee-lay"). In powder form, this spice and thickening agent is made of dried and ground sassafras leaves. Its origin down south is traced to the Choctaw Indians, who pulled the football-shaped leaves from the sassafras tree, dried them on rocks in the sun, then pounded the leaves into a powder. Their original use in cooking was for adding to soups and stews for thickening. All parts of the sassafras tree are useful and fragrant. The bark and roots have been used as the source of a special tea for hundreds of years. The tree's root bark is also used as a flavoring agent in root beer. A spoonful of filé powder may be added to your bowl of gumbo to give an earthy taste.

FRENCH BREAD is enjoyable to accompany your gumbo. A "toe" of the French bread from your favorite boulangerie may be used as a sponge to soak up rich broth. A true French bread baguette is crusty and shaped as a long and narrow loaf. But French bread can also be identified as shorter, plumper and softer, similar to an Italian bread. No matter what type of bread is served on the side, once it becomes slightly stale, it may serve a second purpose. Get out your rum! The unused stale bread can be torn apart in cubes and used to make a delicious dessert known as bread pudding with a rum sauce topping.

GREEN ONIONS (also called shallots). Garnish your hot bowl of gumbo with thinly sliced green onions.

GUMBO Z'HERBES (also Mustard Green Gumbo) was once prepared on Holy Thursday during the Lenten season and served on Good Friday, a day of fasting and abstaining from meat for Roman Catholics. The "seven greens" dish usually included mustard greens, spinach, turnip tops, collard greens or beet tops. In addition, potato cubes could be added to make it more filling. There was an old wives' tale that if you consumed seven greens on Thursday then met seven people on Good Friday, you were in for good luck for the rest of the year.

OKRA. Nicknamed "lady's fingers," the vegetable became a mainstay for many southern dishes. The fuzzy green, somewhat slimy pod when cooked has ties to other plants such as cotton with both members belonging to the mallow Malvaceae family. Surprisingly, the okra blooms a beautiful white flower with a red center that resembles the tropical hibiscus. Aside from adding okra to gumbo for flavor or thickening, okra is also good when fried as a great appetizer. Our third U.S. president, Thomas Jefferson, was multitalented as a government leader, surveyor, savvy gardener and hardcore foodie. He began planting okra at Monticello in 1809. Several okra soup recipes, actually known as "receipts" back then, appeared in Jefferson family manuscripts. One receipt included starting with sautéing chopped onions then slow cooking a soup prepared with tomatoes and okra, which was a precursor to our Louisiana gumbo and was also served on rice.

Potato Salad. It may seem like an acquired taste, but many locals plop a scoop of tangy potato salad in the middle of their dish of gumbo. How did this tradition come about? One theory is that a scoop of cold potato salad dropped into the hot gumbo cools off the whole dish. Another theory is that in the early, simpler days, not every homemaker had an automatic dishwasher, and adding the potato salad directly to the gumbo saved the use of a second bowl to serve the potato salad on the side. Thus one less plate to wash!

Rice. Louisiana ranks as the third-largest rice producer in the United States. The crop of rice was introduced to Louisiana after the Civil War and became an ideal crop in the state due to our rainy, tropical climate. Americans eat approximately thirty pounds of rice per person annually. Not surprisingly, Louisianans enjoy double that amount, likely because of the Cajun dishes that include the basic grain, making its addition a perfect balance to the thick, meaty broth of gumbo. Keep in mind that rice is a key ingredient in numerous other Cajun dishes such as jambalaya, boudin, red beans and rice and rice and gravy. Many cooks use rice cookers to prepare their fluffy rice. These cookers serve a second purpose for keeping boudin warm for next day's breakfast.

Roux (roo) is crucial as the root of many rustic Cajun dishes as a thickening agent for gumbo, also for fricassee and étouffée. *To thine own self be true, when making a gumbo, start with a roux!* It's considered the "heart" of gumbo. To save time, some cooks purchase prepared roux in a jar or dry, powdered roux. The roux may vary in color, depending on preference. Many cooks compare the ideal roux to the color of a brown paper bag, while some prefer the richer hue resembling the color of chocolate. Ingredients are usually equal parts butter and flour or equal parts cooking oil or hog lard and flour. Using hog lard makes the dish full-bodied. This tradition stems from the time when families hosted boucheries and used virtually every part of the pig, including the fat. A successful roux is cooked slowly in a pot and may prove to be a good exercise in building up your arm muscles by continuously stirring with a wooden spoon.

SWEET POTATOES. A sweet potato baked in its own crinkly skin can complement the gumbo as a side dish. The sweet potato has been on the rise as a healthy option, as it is a great source of vitamin B6, iron, potassium and fiber and has virtually no fat. Sweet potatoes are a versatile ingredient in preparing roasted, candied or fried or may be used to fashion a delish dessert. This root vegetable belongs to the morning glory flower family and has been enjoyed in Louisiana for centuries. Sweet potatoes should not be refrigerated unless first cooked. What is the difference between yams and sweet potatoes? In the South, they are often mistaken for each other. A sweet potato is sweeter in taste and has a smooth orange skin with a flesh of orange, white or purple. A yam has a rough, brown scaly skin and white flesh. It is long and cylindrical, often with protruding flesh called "toes." Check your neighbor's garden for the popular variety of Louisiana's sweet potato, namely the "Beauregard," which has a sweet, rich flavor and an orange flesh. An unfortunate bad crop of cotton turned farmers in south Louisiana

Tasso, considered a smoked Cajun ham, is often added to gumbos. *Courtesy of St. Landry Parish Tourist Commission (info@ cajuntravel.com).*

to trying out planting sweet potatoes as a cash crop in the 1930s. Today, Louisiana produces 20 percent of sweet potatoes grown in America.

TASSO is Cajun ham made from pork shoulder, cured in a salt box, heavily spiced and smoked. It's popular for adding a smoky taste to gumbo as well as mustard greens.

TRINITY. The vegetables diced celery, bell peppers and onions, which form the aromatic base of many Cajun dishes. It's also called *mirepoix* in French cooking. Often garlic is added to enhance the mix and may be referred to as the "pope."

QUEEN OF GUMBO

One of the first legends to showcase the illustrious gumbo was Lena Richard, a southern trailblazer of culinary delights. She invited TV viewers into her

The Louisiana moon made of hogshead cheese. *Courtesy of Roby Poché.*

A scrappy Catahoula hound with deep-set yellow eyes hobbled toward Jacques. "Come see, 'cause I live on T-Boy's farm over there," the hound explained, pointing his snout to the right. "If you head this way, there's a pirogue for traveling. Together we may find your fortune down the bayou."

Ducking under Spanish moss draped from trees, the duo skedaddled. Sounds of buzzing grew louder as they came upon a bear with giant paws slapping away honeybees. Clumsily, the hefty bear tumbled down to the bayou and fell, *plop*, into a pirogue. "I'm off to find Mardi Gras beads and other riches, and you'd be mighty strong at paddling," Jacques said, inviting the bear to join the expedition.

Mud splattered as the trio drifted through murky water. A burst of stars above turned into fireflies, zigzagging across the sky to light the travelers' route.

Along the way, a raccoon juggled crawfish for his dinner as his bushy tail swatted at mosquitoes. When he signed up to join the group, he was as happy as when "Jolie Blonde" plays at the *fais-do-do*.

What lurked behind twisted trees as the troop slithered down the snake-like bayou? Poking out from feathery leaves of a cypress tree, a sassy, green-eyed cat wailed. Never before in the swampland have you seen such a crafty cat! Carefully, the bear reached out to welcome the cat into the pirogue, because there's more than one way to spin (never skin) a cat.

> *'Skeeters buzzin',*
> *Catfish jumping,*
> *Hills of cypress knees.*
> *Pink sunsets and white egrets,*
> *Along a bayou breeze.*

Thunder clapped as lightning brightened a stained-glass sky. As the storm was a' brewing, the hapless hunters ran for cover. A rooster with plumes of red and gold approached, puffing up his chest, so proud was he to lead Jacques and his crew. Jumping up and down, the cock-a-doodle-do squawked, "Kuh-Kuh-Kack."

Jacques and Catahoula hound. *Courtesy of Roby Poché.*

What would the elders advise? "Pour you some cane syrup on your lost bread and think it over. Time to think outside the icebox!" As his stomach grumbled, Jacques reminisced about the last gumbo that MawMaw had cooked. He reasoned that the rooster would be an asset to his growing number of explorers.

Mirror, mirror, crystal ball; better find a bed before nightfall. It was time to settle in for forty blinks. As the rowdy rooster steered the fearless friends to a rickety cabin, sounds of hollering came from within. A cluster of robbers counted gold doubloons by candlelight.

"Looky here," exclaimed Jacques. Riches were within arm's reach at last! In the dead of night, Jacques's adventurers circled around the shack. There are times in life when things can go wrong—like if you add tomatoes to your Cajun gumbo! This could be tricky as well, but Jacques kicked off a powerful racket to scare away the robbers, hoping to distract them.

How his fiddle squealed and cried. No one could screech louder than the rooster. The hound howled, the cat screamed, the bear growled and you could hear the chugga-chugga of the raccoon scratching the washboard.

What a deafening uproar! The frightened robbers sped off lickety-split. In their haste, they left the gold scattered on the table. After a good laugh, Jacques gathered the bounty.

"Do I look like I just fell off the poboy truck?" Jacques wondered sheepishly. Likely the robbers would return to the cabin before dawn hoping to retrieve their loot. Jacques schemed up a plan, kinda like when you need to make groceries because you're out of both roux and red pepper.

The bear plunked into the rocking chair. The cat curled up under the table. The hound climbed upstairs. The raccoon wrapped his tail and settled on the back porch. Perched atop the roof, the rooster resembled a weathervane.

Without a care in the world, Jacques fell asleep to dream of his fortune. But all he imagined was PawPaw preaching, "A fool and his money will be last in line at the snowball stand."

Before the light of a new day, one of the robbers crept into the dimly lit house. Before you could say "Atchafalaya" (if indeed you know how), the bandit raced out, all shook up like when you do the zydeco dance.

"Yay yie!" the outlaw whimpered, doubled over in pain as he recounted his dreadful experience to his gang. "First I went to the back porch," says he, "but someone scary pulled out a whip to knock me down." (This indeed was the raccoon with his mighty tail.)

"I snuck into the house to sit in the rocking chair, but an old hairy woman was knitting there and—ouch, ouch—she stuck her knitting needles into me." (And that was in fact the bear with his sharp claws.)

"As I stumbled to grab the bags of gold, there was a *rougarou* under the table who bit me sharply." (Guess who? It was the feisty cat with his toothy smile.)

"Yet I didn't give up but crawled up the stairs. What's more, there was a vagabond who rolled around, knocking me against the wall and had me tumbling down." (This was the Catahoula hound twirling over with his strength.)

"The last straw was a screeching demon, slinking toward me. He spun like a twister while brushing my face with a broom to confuse me." (And that, of course, was the cock-a-doodle-doo fluttering about.)

At last, the robbers dashed away, heading to Holly Beach, without the treasure and nary a slice of hogshead cheese!

Be it ever so humble, there's no place like home—unless you go to the duck camp at Pecan Island.

Perched on a rooftop, the rooster keeps watch. *Courtesy of Roby Poché.*

Under the glow of the Louisiana moon made of hogshead cheese, Jacques's victorious gang shuffled along the trail of red beans to return home, with their newfound riches. The aroma of MawMaw's gumbo drew them in. The chank-a-chank music began as Jacques plucked the fiddle and MawMaw pumped the squeeze box. With *cinq sous* in hand, they had not had so much fun since the Mardi Gras at Tee Mamou.

Tout fini—and that's when the king cake was served!

GLOSSARY

ATCHAFALAYA (a-chaf-fa-lie-ya). Located in south Louisiana, the Atchafalaya Basin is the largest U.S. wetland and swamp

BONHOMME (bon-oum). Good man

CAPUCHON (cap-ooh-shon). Dunce-like hat worn by runners during Courir de Mardi Gras

CATAHOULA HOUND (cat-a-hoo-la). Louisiana's state dog, also known as the Catahoula Leopard Dog

CHANK-A-CHANK. Old way of referring to rural Cajun music

CINQ SOUS (san-sue). French for five cents. A common request from the Mardi Gras runners asking for small change to make a ceremonial gumbo

ÉTOUFFÉE (ay-too-fay). Tangy dish, usually of seafood, which means "smothered" in French

FAIS-DO-DO (fay-dough-dough). Cajun event of dancing

HOGSHEAD CHEESE. Cajun pork "pâté" that really isn't cheese but "meat jelly"

"JOLIE BLONDE." Famous Cajun-French song about a beautiful blonde girl

LOST BREAD (also called pain perdu in French). Breakfast or dessert treat of stale bread soaked in egg batter and fried on both sides

MAKING GROCERIES. New Orleans phrase for grocery shopping

PIROGUE (pea-rog). Cajun canoe

POBOY, or "POOR BOY." French bread sandwich originating in New Orleans with meats or seafood

ROUGAROU (roo-gah-roo). Cajun werewolf

ROUX (roo). Base of many Cajun dishes such as gumbo

SNOWBALL. Shaved ice treat soaked with flavored sugar syrup

TOUT FINI (too-fee-knee). All finished

YAY YIE. That hurts

ZYDECO. Fast-paced music or dance in Louisiana

GOOD EATS AND SIDE TRIPS

Look for chances to take the less-traveled roads. There are no wrong turns.
——Susan Magsamen

Y ou may be hard-pressed to decide which community Mardi Gras adventures to experience as you meander on less-traveled roads. Keep in mind the scattering of other fun-loving sites to experience in the area in case you need an excursion away from the chase of the chicken. Whether your interests range from trying out local dishes, scenic areas, historic sites, music venues, shopping or other points of interest, these "one-of-a-kind" spots are memorable. It's best to verify hours of operation via social media or internet research.

KING CAKES

Think like royalty when you come across the enchanting king cake decorated in colors of green, gold and purple and bedecked with Mardi Gras beads. Known by many names, Twelfth Night Cake or king cake is big business. Coffee room talk and Twitter conversations revolve around who bakes the best. Not only are morsels of this richly dressed cake delicious, but one slice also comes with a prize. Is the taste of the king cake reminiscent of a doughnut or a cinnamon roll? Is it filled with cream cheese? Is the top covered with colored sugar or icing? Serving a king cake has become a ritual

King cake is celebrated during carnival time. *Courtesy of St. Landry Parish Tourist Commission (info@cajuntravel.com).*

for festive occasions during carnival season to celebrate a bridal shower, birthday and many festive occasions, as well as Mardi Gras. These special cakes are treasured for their luscious taste as well as the "good luck" associated with finding the plastic baby in the cake

During carnival, which begins on Twelfth Night or the Epiphany (January 6), bakeries and grocery stores abound with their own variety of the lip-smacking king cake. Most often it is designed as a yeast-based, three-braided coffee cake shaped in an oval ring. Alas, taste-tasting ends on Ash Wednesday, which is recognized as the beginning of the Lenten season, and for the most part, indulgences are curbed.

Once slices for the cake are cut and shared, a frantic search begins for the slice in which the small plastic baby representing baby Jesus is hidden. And the game is on for "Who's got the baby?" The taster with the baby in his cake slice has the honor of buying the king cake for the following week's gathering for everyone to share. Early customs of the New Orleans king cake originated in France, where it is known as *la galette des rois*.

Twelfth Night honors the wise men who visited the manger in Bethlehem at the time of Jesus's birth. During medieval times, part of the celebration of Twelfth Night included serving a cake in which a bean, a coin or even something as extravagant as a golden ring was hidden. Traditions of a king cake associated with choosing a king or queen were later carried over to New Orleans carnival balls. The lucky guest who found the token in his dainty morsel of cake was named lord of the evening's entertainment. This honor also entitled him to command guests to do his bidding, as well as to choose a lady as his queen to accompany him on a musical promenade. Scotland's version of the king cake is known as the "black bun," although it resembles a dark holiday fruitcake and is spiced with whiskey or brandy. In Spain, a king cake is known as *roscon de reyes*.

Following are some bakeries and grocery stores with their own version of the scrumptious king cake.

Champagne's Marché
3802 Highway 31, Leonville

A much-loved spot for heavenly king cakes is Champagne's Marché in Leonville. Nestled along the scenic Bayou Teche and a favored drop-in spot for winded cyclists, Champagne's was built in the mid-1920s. Although known for smoked sausages and tasty plate lunches, Champagne's also prepares twenty kinds of Mardi Gras king cake. One of the most popular flavors is the Amaretto Pecan crammed with sweet filling and the traditional plastic baby. The classic style is of twisted dough made in cinnamon roll style, drizzled with purple, gold and green, which gained Champagne's accolades as no. 1 King Cake in Acadiana in 2015.

When the store was founded by Walter Champagne Sr., it stood across from a blacksmith. The blacksmith structure remains, though horses are no longer shoed at the site. A cotton gin as well as a sugarcane mill were once located in the area.

Many French expressions are shared by patrons wandering through this neighborhood store, which was rebuilt in 1979 and is still family-owned and operated. Walter Champagne Jr. and wife Sarah had a large family of nine children. All were on the payroll and had daily duties to keep the bustling store running. In addition to preparing boudin and stocking shelves, the family stayed busy with watering plants in four greenhouses adjacent to the Champagne family home. It was the foresight of the Champagne patriarch to finance a college education for each of their children.

Today, third-generation store owner Richard Champagne (grandson of Walter and Alma Champagne) and wife Angela oversee the friendly store. How did they get introduced to baking royal king cakes? On a whim, twenty-five years ago, Richard's mother, Sarah, enrolled in a specialty baking class about the art of king cakes. Enthusiastically, she decided to give it a try and began baking a cake or two from her home and used her own mixing bowls and home oven. Once she was satisfied with the results of light and moist cakes, she brought them to the store. Not surprisingly they sold, well, like hotcakes. Family members pitched in to help, and for the first Mardi Gras season, they sold 1,500 king cakes. Now, approximately 3,500 cakes are baked every carnival season. Admittedly, in the early days of the store under Richard and Angela, they had many early mornings and late nights as well to catch up on business of the day. Their children called the store their second "home sweet home," as they hauled in sleeping bags on some evenings to sleep in the store aisles when their parents burned the midnight oil.

RUDDOCK'S BAKERY
556 Northeast Court Circle, Crowley

You always know you're welcome to America's Rice Capital of Crowley. A sign in French proudly thanks you for your visit and suggests that you come back anytime. *Merci de votre visite. Revenez a Crowley.*

Around the historic and quaint town square in downtown Crowley is one of those old-fashioned bakeries that you can stroll to. Customers have even been known to enter the shop dressed in a colorful apron, likely while they are in the middle of preparing Sunday lunch. "I need dessert," the customer exclaims in a panic. Luckily, a cornucopia of sweets is displayed in a glass case. The bakery was originally opened as Huval's Bakery in 1932 by Ernest Huval and was sold to the Ruddocks in 1948. It has changed "hands" or "cookie cutters" of ownership a time or two, though original recipes are still used. The display of vintage kitchen tools adds to the charm of this local fave.

Choose from fruit-filled turnover "hand" pies, moon-sized cinnamon rolls, dreamy cake sold by the slice, chocolate eclairs, meringue pies, brownies for on the go and lots of specialty cookies. It's an icon of treats and sweets. Loaves of French bread are also lined up on oven racks.

A baker's life means kneading and mixing and early starts to the day. Right after the holly/jolly time of Christmas and mini fruitcakes comes another festive carnival season. It's all hands on deck during busy festival time. Glamorous king cakes, formed in an oval shape in a variety of flavors, are flying off the shelf.

RAY'S BAKERY
971 East Laurel Avenue, Highway 190 East, Eunice

Glaze the doughnuts, roll out the cookie dough and get the elephant-shaped cookie cutters ready. Time to take the braided king cakes out of the oven. Let them cool in time for decorating. It takes a whole heap of potholders, mixers, recipes and kitchen timers to run a bakery.

Since 1959, Ray's Bakery has been putting smiles on faces with its "everything's made from scratch" sweets. Ray Oncale started his bakery in 1957 in the small town of Church Point, eventually relocating down the road to Eunice, self-proclaimed Prairie Cajun Country Capital. With business acumen in his background, Ray had helped many family members launch bakeries in Crowley, Lake Charles and Opelousas. Family recipes in hand for cakes, cookies and doughnuts are still used in the mixing bowls. Specials in 1959 for Ray's grand opening were thirty-nine-cent pies and dollar cakes.

Rest Yourself

CRAWFISH HAVEN/MRS. ROSE'S BED AND BREAKFAST
6807 Highway 35, Kaplan
www.crawfishhaven.net

This out-of-the-way spot in Vermilion Parish promises a once-in-a-lifetime experience for both locals and visitors to Cajun Country. Vermilion Parish is known as "The Most Cajun Place on Earth," as nearly 50 percent of the citizens claim Cajun ancestry.

Nestled around Kaplan is a down-home abode where the egrets and mudbugs settle in at Crawfish Haven, also known as Mrs. Rose's Bed and Breakfast.

Built over one hundred years ago, the white clapboard Victorian house is truly a haven extending solitude, though family gatherings are also welcomed. Three bedrooms and three baths offer sleeping for thirteen along with a spacious dining area. The outside kitchen and gazebo accommodate large to-dos like wedding receptions and private parties.

The homestead's wrap-around porch is ideal for guests to sip coffee at sunrise while you count duck hunters en route to their adventure. Or enjoy a glass of wine at sunset and listen to the bullfrogs and other relaxing nighttime sounds.

Catch, cook and sleep in a sportsman's paradise. The private pond in the back allows family and friends to learn the skill of hooking a worm à la Tom Sawyer and reeling in catfish, bream or bass.

Host and innkeeper Barry Toups covers the cooking by expertly whipping up a delectable crawfish omelet, sided with fresh fruit for breakfast along with une *tasse de café* (cup of coffee). Dinner is at your choosing for crawfish étouffée, boiled crawfish or turtle sauce piquante. You might want to pick up one of his compilations of recipes in the *Crawfish Haven Cookbook*.

Barry is a lifelong resident of Vermilion Parish and speaks Cajun-French, which comes in handy, as many guests travel from francophone areas. He offers cooking lessons and will explain about the holy trinity, how to stir a roux and not burn it and the differences between Cajun and Creole gumbo—along with throwing in a few tongue-in-cheek quips about the local culture. Recommendations for local music spots and festivals are freely given.

The retreat is named in honor of Rose Blanchard Robicheaux, who lived in this cozy house for most of her life. She survived many hardships, such as losing her parents and other family members as a result of Hurricane Audrey in 1957. One of her favorite hobbies, aside from nurturing her children, was taking care of her three acres of yard and flower beds. Barry often volunteered to keep the flowers thriving and the yard manicured.

Barry was enthralled by the aura of the farmhouse and decided to purchase it, with no clear plan on how to repurpose it. Originally, he envisioned using it as a makeshift camp and renting it out to duck hunters, as the location was ideal. The idea grew, and Barry reached up to a loftier goal to convert the charming site to a bed-and-breakfast where he would welcome visitors and introduce them to the Cajun experience. He was proud to share the history of the culture, stories of the bayous and scenic drives.

Along the way, he added a private living space for himself, built cypress furniture and fashioned the bed-and-breakfast into a rustic, homey inn with eye-catching artwork, repurposed ladders, unique light fixtures, handmade cypress picture frames with the added touch of crawfish net squares, cypress cabinets (some with use of corrugated tin) and old-style touches to remind you that you are in a house that was built before the Great Depression and World War I.

You may be corrected if you call them crawdads, crayfish or mudbugs. The crustaceans we adore in Louisiana, called crawfish, resemble a little lobster. But we add plenty of spice for this crustacean; 95 percent of all the crawfish eaten in the United States are harvested in Louisiana.

Beginning in 2017, under Louisiana lieutenant governor Billy Nungesser, the life of one lucky crawfish has been saved every year and an official proclamation issued. The likes of crawfish Clyde, Emile and Lafitte have been saved from the boiling pot, treated like royalty and released in a waterway to swim away. And Barry was chosen to select a crawfish to be pardoned from his crawfish pond. The honored crawfish was taken by police escort to the location where Lieutenant Governor Nungesser then delivered his official pardon.

The aura at Crawfish Haven is relaxing, and along with the attentive hospitality offered by Barry, he introduces guests firsthand to the lifespan of Louisiana's favorite crustacean, King Crawfish, from pond to table. With hands-on demonstrations provided by Barry, visitors receive a fascinating lesson on the lifestyle of the crawfish. Guests are invited to ride the ATV along the levee maze through the nearly thirty acres of ponds Barry has cultivated. A narrative is shared of the importance of the water level as well as methods of preventing predators such as otters and raccoons from pilfering the bounty of crawfish from the four hundred pyramid-shaped traps that Barry places in strategic spots annually. Visitors are awestruck by his mention of an alligator that once settled in around the ponds a few years back.

Depending on time of year, houseguests are invited to hop into a skiff and assist with hauling in crawfish nets, hopefully with a full catch of crawfish. Along the way, tips are shared about what's the best bait (pogie fish), how to approximate the age of a crawfish and what to look for to identify the gender.

On the grounds is a back patio, fully stocked with a crawfish boiler and tables set up for eating. Aside from the encounter at the crawfish pond, visitors are invited to watch the process of setting up a boiling pot, adding the right portion of seasoning, and tossing in sides like potatoes, smoked sausage and corn—all part of a crawfish boil to sample this Cajun tradition. Newbies to this feast follow Barry's lead on his technique of the easy way to peel a crawfish; the proper twisting motion of the tail is a good start.

Crawfish Haven has received much attention through social media and accolades from travel expert Samantha Brown. Guests from Japan, Indonesia, France and other locales have been introduced to the Cajun experience here.

Off the beaten path, this unique Louisiana lodging hosts girls' weekends as well as hunters gearing up for a duck and goose hunt.

Restaurants

Suire's Grocery
13923 LA Highway 35 South, Kaplan

It's a treasured hole-in-the-wall spot en route to the islands (Pecan, Forked or Cow). As soon as you jump on the front porch at the entrance, you'll spot the hefty menu hand-printed on the outside. It's called Suire's; it rhymes with beer, and yes, they have that too. Suire's has been a legendary grocery store/restaurant/sweets palace for more than eighty years. Their take on "fine dining" means six tables are set up. Atop each table are a checkerboard as well as a bottle of hot sauce. It's best you go on an empty stomach because the good-sized menu has lots to choose from, whether a poboy, spaghetti, crawfish étouffée or their famous turtle sauce piquante. Do not leave empty-handed, because their counter of sweets is really to die for.

D.I.'S RESTAURANT
6561 Evangeline Highway, Basile

It's truly a destination place, located way out yonder, actually between Bayous Des Canes and Nezpique (Nep-a-kay). D.I.'s stands for owner Daniel Isaac Frugé and his wife, Sherry. In the late 1970s, D.I. was a farmer of rice and soybeans, and Sherry was a hairdresser. They also had a forty-acre crawfish pond.

From pond to boiling pot, D.I. perfected the art of preparing crawfish. He worked hard on weekdays and boiled crawfish. He spread out picnic tables for the locals within the building he used to store tractors and other farm equipment. Through word of mouth, families gathered for D.I.'s juicy crawfish at five dollars for all you could eat.

As the seats filled up each weekend, D.I. saw an opportunity for growing his business. His crawfish was popular, and he needed a building to accommodate his customers, so in 1986 he bought and moved a nearby "catfish shack," complete with a fully equipped kitchen. He renovated it and christened the place D.I.'s Restaurant. Since that time, a bandstand and dance floor have been added on. Expansions of the menu have been made

Mardi Gras masqueraders from Basile dance at D.I.'s Restaurant. *Courtesy of St. Landry Parish Tourist Commission (info@cajuntravel.com).*

as well. You can dine family style with seating for 275, and there are regular performances of live music featuring the likes of Point Aux Loups Playboys, a local favorite.

And for the adventurous, a private 2,900-foot grass airstrip is available for flybys of small planes adjacent to the restaurant. Check with D.I.'s for information about landing, parking and scheduling. D.I.'s welcomes the Jennings Stearman Fly-In (gathering of aircraft) each year during the first weekend in October.

Daniel Isaac Frugé passed away in 2016, and his wife, Sherry Frugé Fudge, and other family members have taken over the helm.

The menu is a seafood lover's paradise, and servings are huge. There's lots to choose from, including dark roux gumbo, BBQ shrimp, frog legs, poboys and famous appetizers such as Angels on Horseback (oysters wrapped in bacon, battered and fried).

When winter comes, it's time to "cut up" during the thrill of Mardi Gras, which takes over the restaurant, as masked costumers of Tee Mamou enter the restaurant to excite spectators. In time to a lively two-step, the runners grab unsuspecting patrons to dance with. Photos of the madcap Mardi Gras performance at D.I.'s Restaurant are scattered throughout this woodsy eatery.

GLENDA'S CREOLE KITCHEN
3232 Main Highway, Breaux Bridge

It's off the beaten path but worth a side trip off I-10 for some top-notch soul food. Glenda's Creole Kitchen has served up "liberally seasoned" heaping helpings of chicken and sausage gumbo during winter-like days since 2000. After you have packed away every spoonful of gumbo, stand by for some home-baked sweets like sweet dough pies. In 2011, Glenda appeared on the Travel Channel's *No Reservations* when Anthony Bourdain stopped by for some sampling.

Her café is postage stamp sized with a couple of tables squeezed in for indoor seating and an outdoor covered patio. Fresh-squeezed lemons are used to make iced lemonade. A good mix of great dishes is served up, such as fried porkchops, seafood on Friday, barbecue ribs and chicken on Sundays, smothered cabbage, white beans, red beans and sausage. Yummy place to drop in and lots of finger lickin' going on.

Cajun Claws Seafood Boilers
175 Frontage Road, Duson

Boiled select crawfish (that means big and bad) as well as shrimp and crabs are a hot commodity. Cajun Claws is a family-oriented woodsy restaurant, but there's a bar, too, to enjoy a Bloody Mary in a starring role. Also on the menu are homemade fried onion rings, poboys and other Cajun specialties. Live music is featured regularly. Remember not to wear a white shirt to a crawfish boil.

Stelly's Truck Stop
8621 US-71S, Washington

It's a truck stop type of casual, homey, mom-and-pop, friendly roadside café/truck stop/grocery store. It's en route to the casino in Marksville or to a deer hunting lease in the environs. A mounted alligator on the wall behind the cash register greets you at this nostalgic truck stop, reminiscent of family road trips from the past. The entrance sports an eclectic inventory of candy cigarettes, work gloves, kids' rubber boots and a display of collectible bottles.

The dining area is unique. Hanging on the walls are seven mounted deer heads, a stuffed bobcat and other wildlife elements. Magnolite pots, cast-iron skillets and other essential Cajun cooking tools are for sale. Choose from tables, booths or an old-time lunch counter for dining. Stelly's is open for breakfast, lunch and dinner. Plate lunch specials are prepared daily.

It's not polite to eavesdrop, but you will have customers coming in from all over to try out the specialty dishes at this nearly one-hundred-year-old gathering spot. So many of the patrons greet each other on a first-name basis. If it's your first visit, you may be asked in a neighborly way if you're from St. Landry Parish or from out of town. This corner of the world has survived the Great Depression and the Flood of 1927 and served as a go-to spot for servicemen traveling during World War II. At one time, a blacksmith shop was located on-site. The eatery began with family preparing sandwiches; they kept improving the menu, and a dining area was added on.

The gumbo is old-school with a generous serving and tastes delicious. Stelly's also offers burgers, poboys (fried shrimp is well-seasoned), fried chicken and other Cajun specialties. Dirty rice as a side to wonderful entrées is good on Sundays. Breakfast means puffy scratch-made biscuits. Adjacent to the café is Stelly's Grocery Store with all cuts of meats.

Patacon Latin Cuisine
308 Bertrand Drive, Lafayette

The namesake of this colorful café stems from a popular type of Venezuelan street food. A *patacon* is a sandwich that uses two deep-fried plantains rather than traditional bread. A plantain is similar to a banana and proves its versatility through baking and frying for an exceptional taste. The sandwich is filled with a creative rendition of shredded beef, chicken, pork, crawfish or shrimp. Stacked high with greens, tomatoes and avocado, the sandwich is completed by a homemade green sauce. Through word of mouth and a successful booth at local festivals, Patacon has quite a following since it opened five years ago to share the riches of Latin America. The *arepa con pollo* is a chicken sandwich where the "bread" is a baked white cornmeal patty. Other specialties include empanadas, *hallacas* (traditional Venezuelan tamales) and *tequeños*. Tempting desserts include tres leches cake and dainty alfajores cookies filled with creamy caramel-like dulce de leche and rolled lightly in coconut.

Cedar Deli
115 Jefferson Street, Lafayette

Cedar Deli was one of the first to introduce kibbe, grape leaves and muffulettas (choice of French or Italian) to Lafayette. The chalkboard of menu items is updated daily with lamb gyro, lentil pilaf, grape leaves and Greek salad. It's in a prime spot, near the college campus, downtown, and behind a popular ice cream shop. Opened in 1981, Cedar Deli specializes in addictive Mediterranean cuisine in a charming spot that now sports an art gallery. Shelves of goods such as tahini, olives, cheeses, chickpeas and other specialties serve as a resource for at-home preparation of family recipes. Mix up your taste buds with an assembly of delicious sandwiches like the specialty of a chicken curry sandwich, gyro and salad and appetizers like baba ghanoush with pita bread.

Boudin Bermuda Triangle in Scott

Boudin is a savory combo derived from a variety of pig parts, including liver and intestine. Once the chopped-up boneless pork meat is cooked, seasoning, onions and prepared rice are mixed in. Boudin resembles a sausage, though

Boudin is a hot and spicy mix of pork and cooked rice stuffed in a sausage casing. *Courtesy of St. Landry Parish Tourist Commission (info@cajuntravel.com).*

it includes the addition of seasonings and rice as filler. It's often served in a brown paper bag and good for breakfast, lunch or a quick snack. Many self-proclaimed carnivorous experts sample varieties to compare the meaty links for color, amount of liver, ratio of meat versus rice portions and even ease in handling. Some boudin aficionados are so attuned to finding the best boudin that they have developed their own family grading scale for spiciness, mushiness and chunkiness.

In 2012, the town of Scott captured the attention of boudin fans when it garnered the prestigious banner of "Boudin Capital of the World" followed by an annual hosting of the Scott Boudin Festival. This town, also known as *la Ville de Cochon* (Pig City) "where the west begins," possibly has the most boudin shops per capita in Louisiana. Each shop right off I-10 has its own fans. The list includes: The Best Stop, NuNu's, Don's Specialty Meats, Kartchner's and Billy's Boudin and Crackling. All of these have boudin, cracklings and other Cajun specialties. The best way to select your favorite is to test out each spot and squeeze the meaty boudin link to compare spiciness and chunkiness.

KARTCHNER'S GROCERY AND SPECIALTY MEATS. It originally opened in 2009 down the road in the town of Krotz Springs on Highway 190 between Opelousas and Baton Rouge. Take your ice chest to stock up on the assortment of specialties in this new six-thousand-square-foot meat market. Known for boudin balls stuffed with jalapeño and cream cheese, there are nine different types of boudin on the counter, plus a gazillion (actually 140) different specialty meats. Most products are available hot, cold or frozen and ready to ship.

NUNU'S. Formerly Earl's, the NuNu's story began at the Blue Room Lounge in the town of Milton. Opened in 1953 by Arthé Broussard, grandfather to the current generation of family owners, the Blue Room Lounge was a popular stop in the afternoons. This country store, with several NuNu's locations in Lafayette Parish, is known for its plate lunches, like Cowboy Stew on Mondays and Pork and Sausage Jambalaya on Saturday.

Don's Specialty Meats. Known for its Sunday BBQ and stuffed breads, it's a slick superstore of quality boucherie meats.

The Best Stop. Known for entertaining visitors on Mardi Gras. Masked runners in full colorful gear drop by the grocery store to roam through the store aisles as wide-eyed visitors are invited to dance. The Best Stop has pork boudin (with liver) as well as chicken boudin with a nice blending of Cajun seasoning.

Billy's Boudin. Known for boudin *pistolettes* and breads as well as crawfish pistolettes. A pistolette is a stuffed and fried bread roll—it's a Louisiana specialty. And try the boudin-stuffed bread.

PJ's Grill
2021 North Parkerson Avenue, Crowley

This casual dining spot has a cool look; attached to the café is a private dining area. The décor was formed from massive rice bins and has made good use of refurbished wood from an old Pennsylvania grain mill. Posted throughout are images and memorabilia about Crowley and the rice industry. This theme is in keeping with the history of the town, which has hosted the Rice Festival for over fifty years. Breakfast at PJ's is the best with a crawfish omelet, homemade biscuits and plenty of sides. Also on the menu for other meals are hamburgers, poboys, salads and a daily "blue plate special." To get your weekend started, try frozen lemonade "the hard way" with hand-squeezed lemons and a shot of locally made rice vodka. Shots of vodka are supplied locally by JT Meleck, which has produced distilled vodka out of rice since 1896 on twenty acres of marshland through four generations of the Frugé family.

Mel's Quick Stop
1894 Veterans Memorial Highway, Eunice

This is the easy stop for bread, milk, eggs, fuel and pork as well as chicken cracklings and boudin. What more do you need? There's a glass display case for meats of every kind—even ponce (pig's stomach), stuffed beef tongue and smoked pork hocks. And the butcher can help you out—the pork hock is meat taken from both the back and front legs. It's considered rich in fats and can be slow-cooked with greens or beans. Weekday plate lunches will fill your tummy. The location is key, since this country store is located near the forty-two-acre Lakeview Park & Beach, a road trip haven for campers. Lakeview offers an old-style lake for fishing and canoeing. Other highlights are the swimming pool and man-made lagoon and beach. Cajun and zydeco musicians perform on Saturday nights in a big barn on the property. Cook-off competitions are also held on a regular basis, such as a winter Beef Tongue Cook-Off—that's not something you find at too many places!

Downtown Eunice

Aside from all the bravado during Mardi Gras, Eunice, known as Louisiana's Prairie Cajun Capital, has a picturesque downtown square and sights to visit.

Cajun Music Hall of Fame and Museum
South C.C. Duson Street, Eunice

This is a free museum where you can visit the likes of pioneer Cajun accordionist Joe Falcon and his singing canary wife, Cleoma Breaux Falcon. Cajun musical instruments from years gone by are displayed. It also features a Wall Hall of Fame with photographs and articles about great Cajun musicians. This museum was created to honor those individuals who contributed to our cultural music and who otherwise may have been forgotten. It's fascinating to view artifacts such as musical instruments, records and albums of Cajun sounds, as well as memorabilia of yesteryear. Also of note on display are the straw hat and rosary of Nathan Abshire. Once a barber, Abshire was a popular singer and songwriter.

Liberty Theater
200 Park Avenue, Eunice

Although it's going through a major facelift, the theater originally opened in 1924 as a silent movie theater and then became a vaudeville house for

Liberty Theater in downtown Eunice originally open in 1924 as a silent movie theater, then a vaudeville house. *Courtesy of St. Landry Parish Tourist Commission (info@cajuntravel.com).*

live performances. It continues as a showcase for live music through a weekly Cajun music and humor radio and TV show. Construction on the building started in 1919 and stalled for about four years because of the financial crisis of 1920. The Liberty plays a leading role in the Eunice Mardi Gras as well.

CAFÉ MOSAIC
South Second Street, Eunice

The Café Mosaic, housed in a building dated to the 1900s, once housed a drugstore and men's clothing store. Coffees, lattes, espressos, calming teas and confections of all kinds are served in this cozy spot. During Mardi Gras season, it serves its own creation of Coffee-Infused King Cake.

LOUISIANA ORPHAN TRAIN MUSEUM
223 S. Academy, Opelousas

With a surge of hundreds of thousands of immigrants coming into the United States in the late 1800s and settling in New York City, overpopulation became a problem. Children lived on the streets, as they were either orphans or their parents could no longer take care of them because of a lack of available jobs. Theologian/philanthropist Charles Loring Brace, through the Children's Aid Society, created an orphan train concept as a humanitarian means to relocate orphans of New York City to other states. Although it seems radical in today's time, the orphan train served as a way to provide good homes, education and jobs for these children. The plan was to take a majority of children off the streets of New York and place them into rural homes across America.

It is considered the largest child migration in the United States. The Children's Aid Society and the New York Foundling Hospital gathered resources to help more than 250,000 homeless or abandoned children living on the streets of New York City. These children, aged infant to teenager, were transported by train from New York City to pre-selected towns in forty-five states, including Louisiana.

The first orphan train traveled from Albany, New York, to the Midwest in 1854. Announcements were made throughout the United States, through posters at general stores or through church services, to entice possible foster parents. Louisiana received two thousand children via the orphan train, and one of the stops was the town of Opelousas. The last orphan train ride to Louisiana was in 1929. It was in that year the program ceased, in large part due to growing measures by state legislatures across the country to restrict or forbid the interstate placement of children.

The museum has a large collection of original documents, clothing and images on display, and many of the museum's volunteers are descendants of orphan train riders. It serves as the only one of its kind in Louisiana and is second in the nation to the Orphan Train Museum in Concordia, Kansas.

ISTRE CEMETERY
Swift Road, Morse

People who enjoy visiting old graveyards are called taphophiles. It's a great setting to take a look into the past. As they wander through rows and rows

Istre Cemetery in rural Acadia Parish is known for its historic grave houses. *Courtesy of Annette Huval.*

of gravesites, these tombstone tourists may spend their time reading the epitaphs, do tombstone rubbings to frame as artwork, take photos or study the surnames of the deceased in hopes of solving genealogy puzzles. In Louisiana, many of the deceased are buried above ground. The theory is that this burial method relates to the challenges of our swampy environment.

The Istre Cemetery, located in rural Acadia Parish, dates back one hundred years and is shaded by majestic oak trees. The pastoral setting is secluded and quiet. This cemetery draws visitors from all over, due to the three distinctive small wooden houses, called locally "little houses" or *les petite maisons*, as that is what they resemble. These gravesites are complete with windows, doors with hinges, painted wood siding and shingled, gabled roofs to enshrine and protect the deceased from the elements of floods, hurricanes and humidity. The height of the grave houses is approximately five feet. At one time, fifty of these grave houses housed the departed.

So treasured are the three remaining grave houses that they were added to the National Register of Historic Places in 2008. Many of the graves are beautified, with vases of flowers, religious statues, votive candles, rosaries, personal mementos and photos to represent family interests.

One of the oldest little grave houses belongs to Pierre Henry, built in 1935, though the name on the grave marker is "Pirrie Henry." Chance Henry, Le Capitaine of the Cadien Toujours organization of Mermentau Cove, serves on the board of the Istre Cemetery. He is among the many volunteers who continue efforts to clean up and preserve the cemetery. Pierre Henry was his great-grandfather's brother. Through family research, it was discovered that the farmland that Chance and his family live on originally belonged to Pierre Henry.

LORRAIN PARISH PARK AND BRIDGE
7803 Lorrain Road, Hayes

This historic bridge is one of Louisiana's oldest wooden drawbridges. It was built in 1895 when the Lorrain family from France headed to the area between the rural communities of Lacassine and Bell City. It was originally built for use of a sawmill and later became an important path for moving cattle for local farmers. The bridge was later reconstructed to connect Calcasieu and Jeff Davis Parish. Lorrain Park and Bridge serves as a mecca for road trippers looking for an off-the-beaten-path scenic locale for a picnic under ancient cypress and oak trees. With care, you may spot gators, turtles and birds. It's a favorite destination for photographers, so take your camera to get some nice contrasting shots of the landscape as the dappled sunlight shines through trees. Fishing in the bayou is another good pastime.

TOWN OF LAKE ARTHUR

Originally an early camping ground for Native Americans, the town of Lake Arthur was named after early settler Arthur Leblanc. The area is much loved for its abundance of wildlife. Fishermen and duck hunters are drawn to the body of water called Lake Arthur, sized one mile by nine miles, which connects with the Mermentau River, a navigable waterway to the Gulf of Mexico. A famous outdoorsman who visited the area on more than one occasion was Franklin D. Roosevelt. He was invited to a sojourn at a popular hunting camp in Lake Arthur. Another frequent visitor was journalism pioneer Dorothy Dix.

NOTT'S CAJUN RESTAURANT
639 Arthur Avenue, Lake Arthur

Dine where the locals do at this unassuming, casual concrete shoebox of a café with seafood delights. The extensive menu has gumbo, ribeye steaks, poboys, eggplant pirogues, fried frog legs and potatoes topped with crabmeat au gratin. "Come again and don't be a stranger" is Nott's motto. Daily plate lunches are available for those on the go who like to fill up on rice and gravy or home favorites like fried chicken or shrimp and egg stew.

REGATTA SEAFOOD AND STEAKHOUSE
508 Hawkeye Avenue, Lake Arthur

For waterfront fine dining along Lake Arthur since 2011, this is the spot to visit, as patrons can watch boats cruising by. You can drive to the eatery or come by boat and walk over for seafood classics like crab cakes, lobsters on Thursday nights, all-you-can-eat fried fish on Fridays or steak specials on Thursday nights. There's also Sunday brunch in this rustic setting. Crafted cocktails can be enjoyed at the Regatta's Sandbar while you relax and enjoy the orange sky at sunset.

TOWN OF JENNINGS

The name of the town derives from an industrious builder of railroad depots in the area in 1882 known as Jennings McComb. However, the actual founding and growth of Jennings is attributed to Sylvester L. Cary. A native of the state of Iowa, "Father" (Sylvester) Cary, as he was often called in recognition for his accomplishments, served as first railroad agent for Jennings under Southern Pacific Company, deacon of the first church, father of the area's rice industry and first teacher of the first school. He tagged the town "Land of Sunshine and Flowers"—as compared to the harsh winter blizzards he experienced in his home state. Much excitement was sparked in 1901, as the Jennings area, specifically at the Jules Clement Field, was the site of Louisiana's first oil gusher. However, a few months after this remarkable discovery, a horrific blaze took over a restaurant and wiped out most of the downtown businesses and homes. Today, the city of Jennings, parish seat of Jefferson Davis Parish, continues to thrive.

JENNINGS CARNEGIE LIBRARY
300 North Cary Avenue, Jennings

A town without a library is like a rose without its perfume, as noted in an early column in the *Jennings Daily News*. Although the first public library in Jennings was developed in 1889 by the sponsorship of the Jennings Ladies Library Association, it burned during the disastrous fire of 1901. Through community efforts, the library was rebuilt by 1907 with assistance from the nationally known Carnegie Foundation. From 1886 to 1919, nineteenth-century industrialist Andrew Carnegie invested in building nearly 1,700 new libraries across America. His goal was to place books in hands to spread the wealth of knowledge. Impressive historical memorabilia, collections and resources are available for viewing by the public.

DARREL'S POBOYS
1002 North Lake Arthur Avenue, Jennings

The casual sports bar has a small menu, enabling the chef to specialize in some mighty well-seasoned, juicy offerings. Seasonally, Darrell's has boiled crabs, crawfish and shrimp. The poboys are bountiful and deliciously messy. The Surf and Turf is a surprising combo of juicy roast beef, topped with Cajun shrimp, which is sautéed in spicy butter sauce and covered with gravy. The café bears local football memorabilia including retro black-and-white photos of the Jennings High School Bulldogs team. Depending on your seating arrangement, you may watch your favorite team on TV.

W.H. TUPPER MERCHANDISE MUSEUM
311 North Main Street, Jennings

The hands of the clock seem to have stopped at the Tupper Museum, a living history museum of a general store. It gives a close-up look into early twentieth-century life in rural Louisiana among French and German settlers who came to the prairieland of Jefferson Davis Parish when the railroad was built.

Jennings boasted a thriving farming community, as by 1885 more than 50 percent of the new settlers were farmers transplanted from Iowa, Kansas and Illinois. The Tupper family farm was located on the outskirts of town, specifically in a rural area called "China." For rural families to pick up their supplies, travel to stores could prove difficult. Visits had to be planned, as farmers had to travel either by horseback, buggy or wagon to come into town. To accommodate the flourishing agricultural community, a blacksmith by trade with a second-grade education named Willis Harvey Tupper built a small general merchandise store on his own farm in 1910. A post office was later added, with Tupper named as postmaster.

A well-stocked general store was essential in a small community to bring in modern conveniences. New services were introduced through the general store, which was usually the first available neighborhood location to share a working telephone with the public.

The store also served as a meeting spot for everyone to get neighborly and compare notes on crops. The smell of coffee beans grinding and a variety of spices greeted customers. Children were drawn to jars of bright penny candy. Ready-made clothing was on display and, for those handy with needle and thread, colorful bolts of cotton fabric and buttons. Gentlemen inspected the newest tools that might make their work easier. Customers were excited to enter the welcoming atmosphere of the store and edge up to the potbellied stove to warm up.

Tupper's stock included groceries, medicines, clothing, hardware, dry goods, fresh milk and a little bit of everything needed to run a homestead. During the Great Depression, workers were often paid with "Tupper chips," which could be used to purchase goods only at the Tupper Store.

As modes of transportation grew and people had more opportunity to get around, the store outlived its usefulness. Although Tupper died in 1936, his daughters, Agnes and Celia, and later their brother, Joseph, kept it going until they closed the store in 1949. Contents of the store, many of which remained in unopened packages, were well-preserved. With the goal to recreate a general store/living history museum of the old days, everything was moved to a building that was the site of the first hardware store in Jennings.

All of the items in the museum are original. Display boxes are filled with toys of yesteryear such as Charlie McCarthy, Betty Field paper dolls, tea sets, bagged marbles and kewpie dolls. On the shelves is an assortment of carefully folded vintage aprons, classic coffeepots, ladies' hats, hair pomade, cigars, the tonic Hadacol and a rare collection of Native American pine needle baskets of the Chitimacha and Coushatta tribes. Many items have the original price tags. The store serves as a wonderful peek into days of the past.

Town of Rayne

Frog Statues

A dandy of a tuxedo-clad giant metal frog tips his hat to all who enter Rayne, home of frog murals and an annual festival. Rayne is considered Frog Capital of the World, and you can drive through town searching for the 110 whimsical statues, which celebrate the *ouaouaron* (wad-ah-ronh), "bullfrog" in French.

In the 1800s, a gourmet chef named Donat Pucheu began selling bullfrogs to New Orleans restaurants as a delicacy. Through transition, Parisian Jacques Weil and his brothers settled in Rayne in 1901 and formed a successful business promoting Rayne as Frog Capital of the World in their advertising. They began exporting skinned frogs to restaurants and universities throughout the United States. Sardi's in New York boasted on its menus of offering "frog legs from Rayne, Louisiana, USA, Frog Capital of the World," bringing acclaim to the little town through the unexpected commodity. The town's downtown is dotted with these uniquely designed frog statues as well as a series of murals in honor of the illustrious amphibian.

ST. JOSEPH'S CATHOLIC CHURCH CEMETERY
400 South Adams Street, Rayne

It is sometimes tagged as Louisiana's only "wrong way cemetery," as noted in *Ripley's Believe It or Not*. In this one-of-a-kind cemetery, the above-ground crypts of the dearly departed face north–south instead of the traditional east–west. It is customary that Christian cemeteries bury their dead facing the rising sun. It wasn't originally planned this way for St. Joseph! In 1880, the entire town of Pouppeville, as Rayne was first called, was disassembled for business reasons and relocated five miles to the north to be closer to the main line of the Louisiana Western Railroad. Among other integral elements of a city block, the cemetery was also moved and interments repositioned for their final resting place in a north–south orientation.

FRED'S LOUNGE
420 Sixth Street, Mamou

The town of Mamou is considered the Cajun Music Capital of the World, mostly because of its iconic Fred's Lounge. This dynamic dancehall opened in 1946 in the center of town. Cajun or zydeco musicians gather every Saturday morning and play their tunes past noon. Alfred "Fred" Tate purchased what was originally called Tate's Bar. In honor of the revival of the Courir de Mardi Gras in the area, Fred's became an informal headquarters for the runners. Fred's has dancers with bodies shaking, arms swinging and hands reaching out to partners to step in tune to the lively music. The dance floor is small, but devotees of the music flow through the maze seamlessly, enjoying every step. Attendance grows from January 1 to Mardi Gras. And yes, alcohol is served (beer and whiskey) early in the day, with honors going to the spicy Bloody Mary. *Allons danser!* Whether Cajun or zydeco music, the energetic beat of the sharp blending of accordion and fiddle entices dancers and music lovers in Cajun Country and way beyond. Whether or not you understand French, you will enjoy the lively music and accompanying bouncing of the dancers spinning the Cajun jig or zydeco shuffle. Cajun music, traditionally sung in French, features the fiddle. In the late 1800s, the accordion was introduced, and the mix, along with the metal triangle, created a fast pace. Be on alert that smoking has been known to take place here, but there's no cover charge to enter. Next to Fred's is a barbershop; two steps down is a bar, then another bar and yet another bar. But Fred's is the only one with live music. Across the street from Fred's is the Krazy Cajun Café, which serves a full breakfast and lunchtime standard fare.

Washington Old School House Antique Mall
123 South Church Street, Washington

Open on weekends for antique fans of everything old is new again, this is the hot spot for vintage wares. The forty-thousand-square-foot two-story building, built in 1936, once served as a school. Now the old wooden floors are graced with linens, toys, books, tools, glassware, knickknacks, artwork, furniture, retro clothing, kitchenware and a hodgepodge of collectibles to suit everyone.

Bayou Rum Distillery
20909 South Frontage Road, Lacassine

Adults will enjoy a tour of how Bayou Rum is crafted in copper pots using 100 percent natural, unrefined Louisiana cane sugar and molasses. These natural resources are provided by an iconic Louisiana sugar mill, M.A. Patout & Sons, which is the oldest family-owned and operated sugar mill in the United States. Enjoy the sampling from Bayou Rum's impressive portfolio of premium spirits. The signature rum is Bayou XO Mardi Gras, with its surprising hints of deep mahogany, tobacco and a burst of black currant and tupelo honey. The tour walks you through stages of fermentation, distillation, maturation, aging in bourbon and sherry casks and hand-bottling.

Mardi Gras Museum of Imperial Calcasieu
809 Kirby Street, second floor, Lake Charles

Stroll through the six rooms featuring feathers, glitter and sequins of elaborate costumes. Experience the sights and sounds of the Mardi Gras aura. Learn about the history of king cakes and climb aboard a float to get the thrill of being in a Mardi Gras parade. As Lake Charles has undergone many challenges during recent hurricanes, it is advised that you call for the museum schedule at (337) 430-0043.

Louisiana Marketshops
I-10 Exit 115, Henderson

This colorful, funky shop features over three hundred Louisiana artists and makers of Louisiana products. It's worth a stop for your Cajun fix at this laid-back shop of three thousand square feet. It houses a plethora of groovy Louisiana art, fine crafts, collectibles, gifts, books, unique yard art, recycled treasures, T-shirts, Christmas ornaments, man-cave/camp/swamp décor, pottery, farmers market items, candles, jewelry and lots of interesting goodies. Browse through selections of a handmade papier-mâché sculpture in design of a shotgun, crocheted voodoo dolls, Cajun music CDs or handmade bamboo chopping boards with a Louisiana theme.

Cajun Country Club
8708 Church Point Highway, Church Point

This dancehall has promoted a wide range of live music since it opened forty years ago. Through many years of being shut down and a recent change of ownership, the club brings in a crowd of dancers. Owner Jazzper Bellard has given the club new life through remodeling and booking zydeco and Cajun bands. Chowdown at noon means a daily plate lunch and trays of boiled crawfish when in season. Pool tournaments are held on Monday evenings.

Bellard has participated as a Mardi Gras captain in full glory. He is committed to keeping the traditions alive. He is a Church Point native and grew up riding horses. During high school, he participated in the rodeo circuit and rode bulls professionally through the PRCA. He has tried his hand at working offshore and two years ago bought and revived the Cajun Country Club. He followed in his father and grandfather's footsteps by riding in the Mardi Gras at age fourteen. He admits that the craziest act he performed during the Mardi Gras run was happily crawling through culverts half filled with water and mud. That act is mild compared to his turns of being thrown off a bucking horse during rodeo training.

Chicot State Park
3469 Chicot Park Road, Ville Platte

Keep your compass in your backpack as you head to this scenic spot for adventurers near the town of Ville Platte (French for "flat town," relating to its flat topography). The 6,400 acres of rolling hills and water of Chicot State Park was added to the Louisiana State Park system in 1939. Several hiking and backpacking trails encircle the 2,000-acre manmade Lake Chicot with vivid outlooks of hardwood forests. As you set up an impromptu picnic in the great outdoors, wild turkeys, pigs, deer, alligator, snakes and raccoon may be spotted. The setting also is a haven for birdwatching. Take your fishing pole to one of the three boat launches, as Lake Chicot has largemouth bass, crappie, bluegill and red-ear sunfish. Canoeing is also popular. Chicot has become a magnet for RV campers, although lakefront cabins are also available for rental. On-site is the Louisiana State Arboretum, which features educational displays and short nature trails pointing out the glories of plant life native to Louisiana.

Town of Grand Coteau

The town of Grand Coteau is situated on what was considered the west bank of the Mississippi River two thousand years ago. Magnificent live oaks form alleys in this *coteau*, French for "sloping ridge." It's a great spot to walk through town, which brags of more than seventy structures designated as architecturally significant. Visit the shrine at the Academy of Sacred Heart, founded in 1821, which was built through the generosity of Mrs. Charles Smith, a wealthy planter's widow, to educate daughters of southern planters.

During the Civil War, the Sacred Heart grounds experienced a large presence of Confederate troops, though the school was not harmed.

In 1866, a miracle was attributed at the Academy of Sacred Heart when a young postulant in the convent was deathly ill. An apparition appeared, making this site one of the documented and Vatican-recognized miracles in the United States. The Shrine of St. John Berchmans, an unadorned chapel where novice Mary Wilson was healed, is available for viewing.

A few blocks away are antique and gift shops like the Kitchen Shop for the buttery dessert of gateaux nana. Several spots in town are of note, including the Church of St. Charles Borromeo, designed by famed New Orleans architect James Freret and built during the late 1800s. Adjacent cemeteries are worth a visit as well.

HIDEAWAY
407 Lee Avenue, Lafayette

Here's a great way to recapture the feel of an old-fashioned Cajun bal de maison at this funky downtown spot for cocktails and a variety of live music genres. Hideaway is the brainchild of musician Wilson Savoy of Pine Leaf Boys and Savoy Family Band, along with David Livingston of Lonesome Whistle Recording, who joined forces during the pandemic to develop the unique venue. In downtown Lafayette, they began major renovations on a 1902 house. The covered patio, porch and indoor seating space give a nostalgic aura that draws musicians such as Wayne Toups, Cedric Watson and Radio Zydeco. Whether Cajun, folk, jazz or zydeco music is your target, Hideaway—with its deluxe burgers—brings in a mix of old and new for a lively evening, complete with a stage and a small dance floor for an intimate concert.

LIVE MUSIC JAMS

One of the most popular draws to Cajun country is the variety of live music available at many venues where impromptu music jam sessions take the stage. What better way to sample the Cajun culture and try out the fast-paced dancing to popular tunes, many sung in French. Usually offering free admission, these casual settings provide musicians the opportunity to collaborate with others. You're welcome to join, so rosin up those bows and start playing. Or just sit back and listen to these family-friendly events.

The most popular music categories are Cajun-French, country, zydeco, jazz, blues and swamp pop. Some musicians play a variety of each.

Cajun French music is as important to Louisiana as a big bowl of gumbo. The cry of the fiddle and wail of the musicians set the stage to nourish and comfort us. Numerous well-rounded musicians perform old favorites as well as original tunes in French. Popular contemporary musicians include T-Monde, FeuFollet, Horace Trahan, Lost Bayou Ramblers, Wayne Toups, Michael Doucet and Pine Leaf Boys. Experts believe that French Canadian immigrants who were transplanted to Louisiana brought ballads they composed, mostly describing the challenges of hardships they experienced. However, since they also lived through joyful times of romance and fellowship, some tunes were upbeat.

Zydeco is a distinctive, fast-paced, jumping up kind of music with French Creole beginnings that often includes the accordion directing the beat along with the scrub board. An early musical influence was Clifton Chenier through his 1965 song "Zydeco Son Pas Sale," meaning "snap beans not salty." In the 1940s, zydeco was fondly known as "la-la" music. Today's popular musicians playing zydeco include Geno Delafose, Terry and the Zydeco Bad Boys, Cedric Watson and Chubby Carrier.

Blues brings in soul and spice to add some unforgettable experiences. Popular blues musicians include Marc Broussard, Tab Benoit and Michael Juan Nunez.

Swamp pop was popularized during the 1950s and '60s as a not-so-gentle blending of rock, pop and rhythm and blues genres performed mainly by Cajun musicians. The Cajun influence is where the term *swamp* comes from, referring to the region where this type of music originated. Legends of swamp pop music include Warren Storm, Tommie McLain and Rod Bernard, as well as contemporary musician Ryan Foret.

Regularly scheduled music jams in Cajun Country include the following:

JENNINGS. SW Louisiana Acoustic Cajun Music Jam at Gator Chateau (exit 64 off I-10), Saturdays (usually first and third weekend, check schedule), 10:00 a.m. to noon. The musicians volunteer their time to play the guitar, drums, accordion and fiddle to entertain visitors. Another worthwhile experience is to drag guests here to caress one of four real gators, which are small and expect to be handled gently. To distinguish between them and their personalities, the gators' nails are painted fancy in a specific color to tag them. Gator Chateau Park includes a small lake and replica of Louisiana's first oil drilling rig. The town of Jennings played a big role in the oil industry, as Louisiana's first oil well was drilled in the area in 1901 in a rice field on the Mamou Prairie.

EUNICE. Savoy Music Center, Saturday mornings. Located on Highway 90. Although wearing shoes is optional, you must learn to tap your toes to the performance of musician Wayne Toups, who is a regular. So in-tuned with each other, the musicians collaborate on what to play and who will take the lead. The beauty of the jam is that a bundle of improvisation takes place.

BREAUX BRIDGE. Tante Marie, Saturday mornings from 11:00 a.m.–2:00 p.m., downtown Breaux Bridge. This artsy café is located in the historic Broussard Hardware building.

LAFAYETTE. Lafayette Farmers & Artisans Market, Saturday mornings from 8:00 to noon at the Moncus Park in Lafayette. Crafts, honey, fresh produce, flowers and more are here for the sampling in this relaxing atmosphere. Try baked goods under the majestic oak trees and enjoy the music.

Vermilionville, third Saturday of the month, 1:00 p.m.–3:00 p.m. Held in partnership with the Cajun French Music Association.

SCOTT. Maison de Begnaud, Friday nights beginning at 6:00 p.m. in Scott at City of Scott's Heritage Visitor Center, a 1907 Acadian house. Enjoy the music and check out the city's memorabilia.

OPELOUSAS. Zydeco Capital Jam at Visitors Center. Monthly, second Saturday of each month beginning at 1:00 p.m.

ARNAUDVILLE. Bayou Teche Brewery, Sundays beginning at 2:00 p.m. on the patio. And don't forget the pizza and brews on tap such as the LA 31 Waking Dead Coffee Kolsch (blonde ale with a coffee flavor roasted with organic Papua New Guinea beans) or the Miel Savage Honey Beer with floral tones of honey, fruit and vanilla.

RECIPES

Cajun cook Camile Resweber Persica has worn many aprons during her lifetime. Like one of her illustrious ancestors, Camile is a determined, somewhat feisty Cajun woman. With roots in St. Martin Parish, Camile is a descendant of Scholastique Breaux, who was the founder of Breaux Bridge.

Camile and her husband, Manuel Persica of Livonia, have catered for large events like crawfish boils, weddings and family reunions and even smaller, intimate get-togethers in Cajun Country for over thirty years. At one time, they owned a roadside destination café between Opelousas and Baton Rouge on Highway 190. Their specialties offer a distinct twist of wonderful, as Camile always has a little something extra up her sleeve.

Camile acquired her culinary skills through creating her own recipes. She enjoys clearing up a few misconceptions about Cajun cooking. It's not about throwing spoonfuls of red pepper in every dish. She emphasizes that seasoning should enhance, and never override, the taste of the prepared meal. She prefers to layer flavors, as she often slow-cooks what's brewing on the stove. Fresh ingredients, preferably from your own home garden or herb boxes, are key. You don't need to have shelves stacked with utensils and pots. A start to simplifying your array of tools is by stocking up with a good Dutch oven and cast-iron pots, wooden spoons and sharp knives. Among her treasured keepsakes is her assortment of black iron pots of various sizes, acquired from generations of family cooks. She recommends stocking up your pantry with cayenne pepper, Cajun seasoning mix, black pepper, salt and bay leaves.

The trinity of bell peppers, onions and celery are a common start for many Cajun dishes. *Courtesy of St. Landry Parish Tourist Commission (info@cajuntravel.com).*

One of her many favorite dishes is Maque Choux, a classic recipe of corn and peppers sautéed until softened. A bit of Cajun seasoning makes it an ideal side dish to gumbo because it's quick to prepare. Many ingredients can be harvested straight from your garden, such as corn, peppers and tomatoes. When preparing the corncobs, scraping the corn kernels, pulp and milk is important to make the finished dish creamy. Maque Choux, a quick staple, is of Native American origin from a dish called *sagamite*, which was maize stewed in bear oil, succotash and fried cornmeal. Maque chou may also be served as an entrée on its own by adding smoked sausage, shredded chicken, bacon or shrimp.

Maque Choux (mock shoe)

4 ears fresh shucked corn
¼ cup vegetable oil
1 large onion, chopped
1 large bell pepper, chopped
1 garlic clove, minced
2 large tomatoes, peeled and diced
Black pepper, salt, Cajun seasoning—to taste

Using a sharp knife, slice off the corn kernels, pulp and corn milk from corncobs. In a black iron pot, add the vegetable oil to sauté onions, bell pepper and garlic until softened. Add corn kernels and diced tomatoes and cook until tender. Season to taste. Cover the pot, simmer for 20 minutes, and continue to stir frequently until corn is tender. Optional: add a small amount of cream for richness.

▾ ▾ ▾ ▾ ▾

Stuffed Bell Peppers
Courtesy of Barry Toups, Crawfish Haven/Mrs. Rose's Bed & Breakfast Cookbook

12 bell peppers
16 ounces frozen seasoning mix of onions, bell peppers, parsley
½ cup olive oil
1 pound Louisiana crawfish tails, chopped
1 pound Louisiana shrimp, peeled, deveined and chopped
½ pound Louisiana crabmeat
½ cup breadcrumbs
3 eggs, beaten
Crawfish Haven seasoning to taste
1 lemon

Cut bell peppers in half, lengthwise, and remove all seeds. Sauté seasoning blend in olive oil. Cook until soft. Add chopped seasoned seafood, breadcrumbs and eggs and mix well. Scoop stuffing in bell peppers and bake in 325-degree oven for 30 minutes. Remove from oven and squeeze lemon juice over top before serving.

▾ ▾ ▾ ▾ ▾

Classic Oven-Baked Beef & Pinto Bean Tacos
Courtesy of Camellia Beans

10–12 hard taco shells
2 teaspoons vegetable oil
½ cup diced onion
3 garlic cloves, minced

1 pound ground beef or ground turkey
1 tablespoon chili powder
¼ teaspoon garlic powder
¼ teaspoon onion powder
¼ teaspoon dried oregano
½ teaspoon smoked paprika
1 ½ teaspoons ground cumin
½–1 teaspoon salt
1 teaspoon black pepper
½ cup water
1–2 cups cooked Camellia Brand Pinto Beans
2 cups shredded sharp Cheddar cheese
1 ½ cups shredded lettuce
1 jar of your favorite salsa
1 container of sour cream

Preheat oven to 400 degrees. Arrange the taco shells inside a 9"x13" baking dish. Heat oil in a large skillet over medium-high heat. Add onion, garlic and ground meat, breaking it up with a spoon, and cooking for 5–8 minutes until browned. Add chili powder, garlic powder, onion powder, oregano, smoked paprika, cumin, salt, pepper, ½ cup water and cooked pinto beans and simmer for a few minutes.

Divide meat and bean mixture among taco shells and top with all of the cheese. Bake for 10 minutes or until cheese is melted and taco shells are lightly browned. Remove from oven. Top tacos with lettuce, salsa and sour cream, and serve immediately.

▾ ▾ ▾ ▾ ▾

Crawfish Burgers
Courtesy of Barry Toups, Crawfish Haven/Mrs. Rose's Bed & Breakfast Cookbook

½ stick plus 1 tablespoon of butter
½ medium onion, chopped
½ cup chopped celery
2 cloves garlic, minced
2 tablespoons mayonnaise
2 teaspoons Worcestershire sauce

1 ½ tablespoons Crawfish Haven seasoning
1 large egg, lightly beaten
30 saltine crackers, crushed
1 pound Louisiana crawfish tails, chopped
3 tablespoons olive oil

In saucepan, melt ½ stick of butter on medium-high heat. Add onions, celery and garlic, stirring occasionally until vegetables are tender, about 10 minutes. Transfer mixture to large bowl. Stir in mayonnaise, Worcestershire sauce, Crawfish Haven seasoning, egg, crushed crackers and crawfish. Mix well and refrigerate for up to at least 4 hours or overnight. Shape mixture into 6 patties. In large nonstick skillet, melt 1 tablespoon butter and 3 tablespoons olive oil on medium to high heat. Cook patties 4–5 minutes on each side.

▾ ▾ ▾ ▾ ▾

How to Make a Roux
Courtesy of Jeff Davis Parish Tourism Commission

⅔ cup flour
¾ cup vegetable oil

A heavy pot is a must to make a pretty roux. Before you start your roux, start heating water in a kettle, the amount depending on whether you are making a gumbo or stew. You must always add hot water (not cold water) to a roux as it could curdle the roux or separate the flour and water from the oil. The measurements given make a roux large enough for a stew with one hen or a gumbo with two pounds of shrimp. To increase recipe, adjust proportions given. It is important to use more oil than flour.

Mix the flour and the oil in a heavy iron pot until it is thoroughly mixed before you turn on the fire under the pot. After it is mixed, turn the fire on medium to low, stirring constantly. Stir all over the bottom of the pot to be sure no particles stick to the bottom. As you stir, the roux browns slowly. Don't cook the roux fast, because as it reaches the done point, it will be too hot and burn as it keeps cooking. When your roux is a rich, dark brown, cut off your fire immediately and continue stirring. Add hot water to lower the temperature slightly so the roux will stop browning. Some people add chopped onions to lower the temperature. Either way, continue to stir until the temperature is lowered sufficiently. Then you may turn your fire on again and add the rest of the ingredients for your stew or gumbo, slowly.

▾ ▾ ▾ ▾ ▾

Gumbo
Courtesy of Jeff Davis Parish Tourism Commission

4–5 quarts of water
2 large onions, chopped
½ bell pepper, chopped
2 cloves garlic, minced
Large hen, duck or goose
1 pound sausage
Prepared roux
1 cup onion tops
1 cup parsley
Salt and pepper, to taste

Bring water to boil in a gumbo or large stockpot. Add onions, bell pepper and garlic. Allow vegetables to cook for about 15 minutes, then add your choice of meat that has been cut into serving sizes. Bring water back to a boil, then add the roux. Let this boil for 30 minutes, but don't let it boil over! Turn down the fire to simmer and cook until meat is tender, for approximately 90 minutes. Add green onion tops and parsley 10 minutes before serving. Serve over hot, cooked rice; sprinkle filé (pronounced "fee-lay") over the gumbo. Add hot sauce to taste.

Variation
1½ pounds shrimp peeled and deveined with 1 pound crab meat and 1 pint oysters may be used to make a seafood gumbo. The roux and water must boil for at least 30 minutes along with the vegetables and be allowed to simmer for 30 minutes longer before the seafood should be added. Add green onions and parsley as directed above. Serve in gumbo or large soup bowls over hot, cooked rice.

. . . . .

Satsuma Blueberry Lemonade Cocktail
Courtesy of Bayou Rum Distillery, Lacassine, LA

1–2 shots of Bayou Satsuma Rum
8 ounces of Simply Blueberry Lemonade

Slowly, add the rum to a glass of Simply Blueberry Lemonade on ice. The hint of blue makes it sizzle.

. . . . .

Bayou Eggnog
Courtesy of Bayou Rum Distillery, Lacassine, LA

1 ½ ounces Bayou Spiced Rum
Top with Eggnog

Pour the drink into cups. Sprinkle the tops with a dash of cinnamon and add a cinnamon stick for decoration. Tis the season year-round.

. . . . .

Jack's Hunter Stew
Courtesy of Louisiana Sweet Potato Commission

1 ½ pounds sweet potatoes peeled and cut into ½-inch cubes (about 3 medium)
¼ cup butter
1 pound venison sausage, cubed
1 cup chopped sweet onion
12 ounces brussels sprouts
4 cups beef broth
4 cups chicken broth
2 tablespoons Worcestershire sauce
1 tablespoon dried thyme
⅛ teaspoon browning and seasoning sauce, such as Kitchen Bouquet
2 tablespoons arrowroot
Salt
Ground black pepper

Soak sweet potato in ice water for 10 minutes. Drain and microwave on high until softened, 7 to 10 minutes. In a stockpot, melt butter over medium heat. Add sausage and onion and cook, stirring occasionally, until onion is softened, about 10 minutes.

Chop half of the brussels sprouts and halve remaining. Add brussels sprouts to venison mixture and cook, stirring occasionally, 10 minutes more. Stir in beef broth, chicken broth, Worcestershire sauce, thyme and browning and seasoning sauce. Bring to a boil, reduce heat and simmer 15 minutes. In a small bowl, place arrowroot. Transfer 1 cup broth from pot to arrowroot and stir until dissolved. Add mixture to stew. Stir in sweet potatoes. Add salt and pepper to taste. Simmer until thickened slightly, about 20 minutes. Remove from heat and let cool 10 minutes before serving. Makes 6 servings.

▾ ▾ ▾ ▾ ▾

Sweet Potato Bread Pudding
Courtesy of Louisiana Sweet Potato Commission

1 stick (8 tablespoons) butter
1 loaf soft French or Italian bread, torn into large pieces
3 medium sweet potatoes
4 cups milk
4 eggs
1 cup sugar
1 teaspoon vanilla extract
1 teaspoon ground cinnamon

Preheat oven to 400 degrees. Butter a medium baking dish with 1 tablespoon butter. Arrange bread cubes in a single layer in the prepared dish and set aside at room temperature to dry out slightly, about 2 hours. While bread is drying out, prick sweet potatoes in 4 or 5 places with the tines of a fork and bake on a baking sheet until soft, about 1 hour. Set aside until cool enough to handle, then halve lengthwise and scoop pulp out of skins. Break pulp into large pieces. Tuck sweet potato pieces between the pieces of bread, mashing them down slightly with a fork.

Beat together milk, eggs, sugar, vanilla and cinnamon in a large bowl. Pour over bread and sweet potatoes and set aside until bread soaks up milk mixture, 2–3 hours. Preheat oven to 375 degrees. Cut the remaining 7 tablespoons butter into small pieces and scatter over bread pudding, then bake until custard is set, 35–40 minutes. Set aside to cool for at least 30 minutes before serving warm or at room temperature.

▾ ▾ ▾ ▾ ▾

Bourbon Praline Sauce

16 tablespoons butter (2 sticks)
¾ cup of light brown sugar
1 cup of chopped shelled pecans
¼ cup of bourbon

Melt butter in a medium, heavy-bottomed saucepan over medium heat. Add sugar and stir with a wooden spoon until sugar melts and mixture begins to boil, about 5 minutes. Stir in pecans and bourbon. Spoon warm sauce over bread pudding.

▾ ▾ ▾ ▾ ▾

Caribbean Sweet Potato Bread
Courtesy of Louisiana Sweet Potato Commission

1 (15-ounce) can sweet potatoes (yams) drained and mashed or 1 cup fresh sweet potatoes, cooked and mashed
4 large eggs
¼ cup vegetable oil
¼ cup Lawry's Caribbean Jerk Marinade with Papaya Juice

⅓ cup water
½ teaspoon vanilla
1 (80-ounce) can crushed pineapple, well drained
1 (1 pound, 2.5 ounces) package yellow cake mix
½ teaspoon cinnamon

In large bowl, beat together sweet potatoes and eggs until fluffy. Stir in remaining ingredients and beat on medium speed with mixer for 2 minutes. Spray two 4x8-inch loaf pans with nonstick cooking spray;

pour half of batter into each pan. Bake in preheated 375-degree oven until toothpick inserted in center comes out clean, about 35 to 40 minutes. Makes 2 loaves.

· · · · ·

Southern Fried Okra Hushpuppies
Courtesy of the Huval family

2 beaten eggs
2 tablespoons buttermilk
1 cup cornmeal
1 cup flour
Cajun seasoning
2 pounds okra
Oil for frying

A wet batter in one bowl can be made by using beaten eggs and buttermilk. In a separate bowl, mix cornmeal, flour and Cajun seasoning. Wash the okra and cut off the tops. Slice the okra into medallions. Dip okra slices, whether fresh or frozen, in the wet egg batter. Dip into the dry batter then deep fry until golden. A side cup of ranch salad dressing adds some zing for dipping the fried okra hushpuppies into.

· · · · ·

Cowboy Caviar
Courtesy of Camellia Beans

Dressing
⅓ cup red wine vinegar
4 tablespoons olive oil
4 cloves garlic, minced
2 teaspoons cumin
2 teaspoons salt
1 teaspoon dried oregano
Tabasco to taste

Salsa
4 cups cooked Camellia Brand Blackeye Peas
2 Roma tomatoes, diced
1 yellow bell pepper, seeded and diced
½ large red onion, diced
1 jalapeño pepper, seeded and finely diced
1 bunch cilantro, chopped

Combine dressing ingredients in a small bowl and whisk together. Add hot sauce to taste. Combine salsa ingredients in a large bowl and toss thoroughly. Pour dressing over salsa and mix gently. Cover and refrigerate for at least 1 hour or overnight. Serve as a side dish or with chips as an appetizer.

▾ ▾ ▾ ▾ ▾

Bean Soup with Pasta (Pasta e Fagioli)
Courtesy of Camellia Beans

1 ¼ cups Camellia Brand Great Northern Beans
5 cups water
1 onion, chopped
1 tomato, chopped
2 celery stalks, sliced
2 cloves garlic, chopped
¼ pound salt pork, chopped
2 teaspoons instant beef bouillon
¼ teaspoon black pepper
½ teaspoon salt
½ cup uncooked Dagostino Birdseye Pasta
Grated Parmesan cheese

Rinse and sort beans. In a Dutch oven, bring water and beans to a boil for 2 minutes. Remove from heat; cover and let stand 1 hour.

Add next 7 ingredients to beans. Bring to a boil, then reduce heat, cover and simmer until beans are tender, about 2 hours. Add salt and pasta; stir. Cover and simmer until pasta is tender, about 10–15 minutes. Serve sprinkled with cheese. Serves 5.

. . . . .

Spicy Sweet Potato Hummus
Courtesy of Camellia Beans

2 cups prepared hummus
2 small sweet potatoes, baked
½ teaspoon smoked paprika
¼ teaspoon cayenne pepper, or to taste
A few shakes Tabasco brand Chipotle Pepper Sauce or chipotle powder

Add all ingredients to the bowl of a food processor or blender and blend until smooth. Adjust seasonings to your taste. Spread on a turkey sandwich or serve with tortilla chips, pita or crackers.

. . . . .

Crawfish Bread
Courtesy of Louisiana Office of Tourism

¼ cup olive oil
¼ cup butter (½ stick)
1 cup chopped green onions (tops and bottoms)
½ cup finely chopped celery
¼ cup finely chopped green bell pepper
¼ cup finely chopped red bell pepper
4 cloves finely chopped garlic
¼ cup white wine
1-pound peeled Louisiana crawfish tails, with fat
8 ounces cream cheese, cut into small squares
Cajun seasoning, to taste
1 (11-ounce) roll refrigerated French bread dough
8 ounces shredded mozzarella cheese

Preheat oven to 350 degrees. In a large skillet, sauté chopped vegetables in olive oil and butter until wilted, about 5 minutes. Add crawfish tails and wine; stir ingredients well and add cream cheese. Stir until cream cheese is melted. Add Cajun seasoning and cook until all is thickened, just a few minutes. Remove from heat, cool and let flavors blend.

Carefully roll out French bread dough on a greased baking sheet. Sprinkle with half of the shredded cheese. Spoon crawfish mixture onto center of dough. Sprinkle on remaining shredded cheese, reserving 1 tablespoon. Fold dough over mixture and tuck ends under to make a loaf. Use the remaining tablespoon of cheese to sprinkle on top. Cut 5 to 6 small slits in dough across the top of the loaf. Bake about 20 minutes at 350 degrees or until loaf is golden brown. Remove from the oven. Allow bread to set for a few minutes. Slice into serving-size pieces. Serves 5 to 6.

▾ ▾ ▾ ▾ ▾

Blackened Catfish with Crawfish Étouffée
Courtesy of Louisianaseafood.com
Provided by D.I.'s Restaurant, Basile, LA

Catfish
2 (7–9 ounce) fresh catfish filets
8 tablespoons of butter, melted
Your favorite blackened seasoning, to taste
1 spray-can of vegetable oil

Crawfish Étouffée
1 large onion, chopped
1 medium bell pepper, chopped
1 stalk celery, chopped
½ pound butter
2 tablespoons flour
1 tablespoon tomato paste
Salt and pepper, to taste
1 to 1 ½ cups of water
1 pound crawfish tails
½ cup green onions

Prepare the catfish by dredging each filet in 4 ounces of melted butter. Coat with blackened seasoning to taste. Place in a hot, heavy iron skillet that has been sprayed with vegetable oil.

Brown each side for about 7 minutes. Serve with crawfish étouffée on top. (Recipe follows.)

To prepare the crawfish étouffée: In a medium sized pan, sauté the onion, bell pepper and celery in the butter until they are tender or clear. Add the flour and stir until the roux has a blond color. Add the tomato paste; mix well. Add the salt, pepper, 1 cup of water and crawfish tails. Simmer for about 10 minutes. Adjust consistency with the remaining ½ cup of water if necessary.

▾ ▾ ▾ ▾ ▾

Pasta & White Bean Salad
Courtesy of Camellia Beans

½ pound Dagostino Shell Pasta
1 cup cooked Camellia Brand Great Northern Beans or Navy (Pea) Beans
½ cup yellow and red grape tomatoes, sliced
½ cup Cheddar cheese cubes
½ cup raw or cooked broccoli florets
1–2 tablespoons extra virgin olive oil
Salt and pepper to taste

Cook pasta according to package directions. Drain and set aside to cool. Add all ingredients to a large mixing bowl and toss well. Season to taste. Serve room-temperature or chilled.

▾ ▾ ▾ ▾ ▾

Sweet Potato Ice Cream
Courtesy of Louisiana Sweet Potato Commission

1 (14-ounce) can sweetened condensed milk
2 (12-ounce) cans evaporated milk
1 quart heavy cream
1 tablespoon vanilla
10 egg yolks
2 cups sugar
1 cup firmly packed brown sugar
1 teaspoon ginger
1 teaspoon cinnamon
¼ teaspoon nutmeg

1 pound mashed sweet potato
1 cup chopped pecans

In a medium saucepan, bring milks, cream and vanilla to a boil over medium-high heat. Meanwhile, in a medium bowl, whisk egg yolks, sugar, ginger, cinnamon and nutmeg until smooth. Gradually whisk cream mixture into egg yolk mixture while whisking to avoid cooking the eggs. Add sweet potato mash and place bowl over a pot with boiling water, stirring constantly, until it thickens and coats the back of a spoon (do not boil or it will curdle). Remove saucepan from heat; refrigerate custard until well chilled, at least 2 hours, but no more than overnight. Freeze in ice cream maker as directed by manufacturer. Just before mixture begins to freeze, add the chopped pecans.

▾ ▾ ▾ ▾ ▾

Lagniappe—Recommendations

TRINITY is the diced celery, bell peppers and onions that form the aromatic base of many Cajun dishes. It's also called mirepoix in French cooking. Often garlic is added to enhance the mix and may be referred to as the "pope." With much experimenting, the dehydration of trinity vegetables was developed as a cottage business in Youngsville. Dreux and Monique Barra loved having a home garden. When they ended up with a good season and a surplus of bell peppers, they looked for a way to make use of the vegetable as well as other key vegetables in the blend of onions, celery, bell pepper and garlic. They developed C'est Tout, a dried trinity mix that does not need refrigeration and has a shelf life of two years. The mix maintains its bold flavor, which is important in cooking Cajun dishes, and saves time, as sautéing is not necessary. It is suitable for adding right into the gumbo pot. www.thisiscajun.com.

FILÉ (pronounced "fee-lay") powder is a spice and thickening agent made of dried and ground sassafras leaves. Its origin down south is traced to the Choctaw Indians, who pulled the football-shaped leaves from the sassafras tree, dried them on rocks in the sun and then pounded them into a powder. Their use was believed to add to soups and stews for thickening. All parts of the sassafras tree are versatile. The bark and roots have been used as the source of a special tea for hundreds of years. The tree's root bark is also used as a flavoring agent in root beer. Or to boost the earthy flavor to gumbo, a spoonful of filé powder can be added. Paul Leleux and his team of Acadian Kitchens in Broussard, Louisiana, blend a variety of seasonings, including their own fusion of filé powder. Acadian Kitchens also produces jalapeño relish, roux, Cajun seasonings, fish fry and seafood boil mix. www.acadiankitchens.com.

BIBLIOGRAPHY

Aloian, Molly. *Mardi Gras and Carnival*. New York: Crabtree Publishing, 2010.

Ancelet, Barry Jean. *Cajun Country*. Jackson: University Press of Mississippi, 1991.

———. *Capitaine, Voyage Ton Flag: The Tradicional Cajun Country Mardi Gras*. Lafayette: University of Southwestern Louisiana, 1989.

Bose, Alan. *The Acadian Kitchen: Recipes from Then and Now*. Vancouver, CAN: Whitecap, 2018.

Broussard, Jeremy. *Grave House Legends*. Lafayette, LA: Corvus Press, 2000.

Cajun Cuisine: Authentic Cajun Recipes from Louisiana's Bayou Country. Lafayette, LA: Beau Bayou Publishing Company, 1985.

Costello, Brian J. *Carnival in Louisiana*. Baton Rouge, LA: Louisiana State University Press, 2017.

Curry, Dale. *Gumbo*. Chapel Hill: University of North Carolina Press, 2015.

Edge, John T. *The New Encyclopedia of Southern Culture*. Vol. 7, *Foodways*. Chapel Hill: University of North Carolina Press, 2007.

Fontenot, Mary Alice. *Acadia Parish, Louisiana*. Vol. 1, *A History to 1900*. Baton Rouge, LA: Claitor's Publishing, 1976.

———. *Mardi Gras in the Country*. Gretna, LA: Pelican Publishing, 1995.

Gaudet, Marcia, and James McDonald. *Mardi Gras, Gumbo, and Zydeco: Readings in Louisiana Culture*. New York: American Heritage Custom Publishing, 1996.

Istre, Elista. *Creoles of South Louisiana*. Lafayette: University of Louisiana Press, 2018.

Kane, Harnett T. *The Bayous of Louisiana*. New York: Bonanza Books, 1943.

Lindahl, Carl, and Carolyn Ware. *Cajun Mardi Gras Masks*. Jackson: University Press of Mississippi, 1997.

Richard, Zachary. *The History of the Acadians of Louisiana*. Lafayette: University of Louisiana at Lafayette Press, 2013.

Tallant, Robert. *Mardi Gras As It Was*. Gretna, LA: Pelican Publishing, 1994.

Tipton-Martin, Toni. *The Jemima Code: Two Centuries of African American Cookbooks*. Austin: University of Texas Press, 2015.

Twain, Mark. *Life on the Mississippi*. Boston: J.R. Osgood, 1883.

Weber, Bea, and Floyd Weber. *The Louisiana Gumbo Cookbook*. Lafayette, LA: Acadian House Publishing, 1998.

Wells, Ken. *Gumbo Life*. New York: Norton & Company, 2019.

Wulf, Andrea. *Founding Gardeners: The Revolutionary Generation, Nature and the Shaping of the American Nation*. New York: Alfred A. Knopf, 2011.

ABOUT THE AUTHOR

ixie Poché is a graduate of the University of Louisiana–Lafayette in journalism. She is a travel and corporate writer in Lafayette and author of three other books about the Cajun culture: *Classic Eateries of Cajun Country*, *Louisiana Sweets* and *The Cajun Pig*, all published by American Palate, a division of The History Press. She enjoys doing research at the lunch counter and discovering Louisiana's hidden gems. She spends time with lots of Cajun cousins hanging out on the front porch.

Visit us at
www.historypress.com